BEVERLY MASSACHUSETTS

ROCKPORT PUBLISHERS

1000 GREETINGS

creative correspondence designed for all occasions   PETER KING & COMPANY

First published in the United States of America by
Rockport Publishers, a member of
Quayside Publishing Group
100 Cummings Center
Suite 406-L
Beverly, Massachusetts 01915-6101
Telephone: (978) 282-9590
Fax: (978) 283-2742
www.rockpub.com

ISBN-13: 978-1-59253-481-4
ISBN-10: 1-59253-481-3

10 9 8 7 6 5 4 3 2 1

Printed in China

THANKS TO THE MANY WHOSE INSPIRING CREATIVITY AND DILIGENCE MADE THIS BOOK POSSIBLE.

CONTENTS

GREETINGS

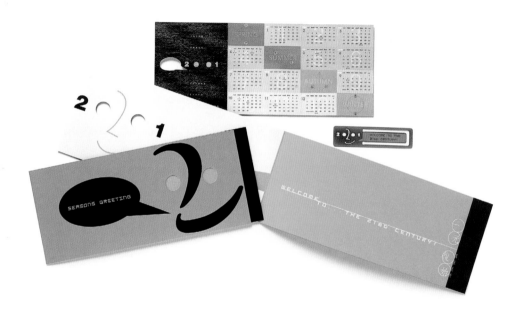

0001 Tong Design Graphic Studio
DESIGN: Tong Wai Hang

**TRULY
MADLY
DEEPLY**

**30
ISH**

 2 0 0 3

IT'SKINGKAMEHAMEHADAY!

JUNE 11 IS THE ONLY ROYAL HOLIDAY ESTABLISHED DURING
THE HAWAIIAN MONARCHY AND OBSERVED CONTINUALLY SINCE
ITS ESTABLISHMENT BY ROYAL PROCLAMATION IN 1871. THE
DAY IS CELEBRATED TO HONOR KING KAMEHAMEHA WHO UNI-
FIED THE HAWAIIAN ISLANDS AND WHO STANDS AS SYMBOL OF
HAWAIIAN SELF-DETERMINATION, *reminding me of my
own determination to say, well, aloha.*

0010 | Chermayeff & Geismar, Inc.
DESIGN: Steff Geissbuhler

We wish you happy holidays and a great and healthy One

Ben, Alex, Elissa & Steff Geissbuhler

0011 Chermayeff & Geismar, Inc.
DESIGN: Steff Geissbuhler

| 0012 | **DESIGN:** Palm Press | 0014 | David Clark Design
DESIGN: David Clark |
| 0013 | Indian Hill Press
DESIGN: Daniel A. Waters | 0015 | Indian Hill Press
DESIGN: Daniel A. Waters |

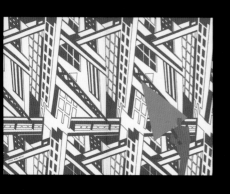

(best wishes from the viñas family: jaime, ghislaine, rice aubel & arabia fynn)

love&peace

'03

0020   Viñas Design
DESIGN: Jaime Viñas

0021

Finished Art, Inc.
DESIGN: Li-Kim Goh, Marco DiCarlo, Luis Fernandez

| 0022 | **DESIGN:** Carolynn DeCillo | 0023 | Voice
DESIGN: Scott Carslake | 0024 | **DESIGN:** Michael Osborne Design |

| 0025 | Joao Machado Design Lda
DESIGN: Joao Machado | 0027 | Miro Design
DESIGN: Judy Glenzer |
| 0026 | Damion Hickman Design
DESIGN: Damion Hickman | 0028 | Miro Design
DESIGN: Judy Glenzer |

Wishing you a year filled with radiance and reflection

DanielsDesign, Inc.
Helping to polish business images since 1969

0029 Daniels Design, Inc.
DESIGN: Larry Daniels

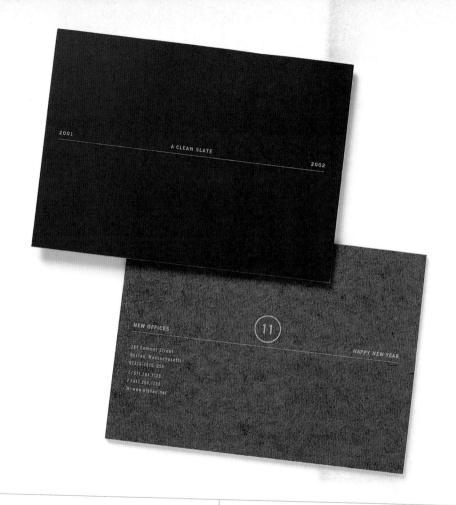

2001

A CLEAN SLATE

2002

NEW OFFICES

281 Summer Street.
Boston, Massachusetts
02210-1510, USA
T / 617.204.1108
F / 617.204.1108
W / www.eleven.net

(11)

HAPPY NEW YEAR

0030   Rick Rawlins/Work
       DESIGN: Rick Rawlins

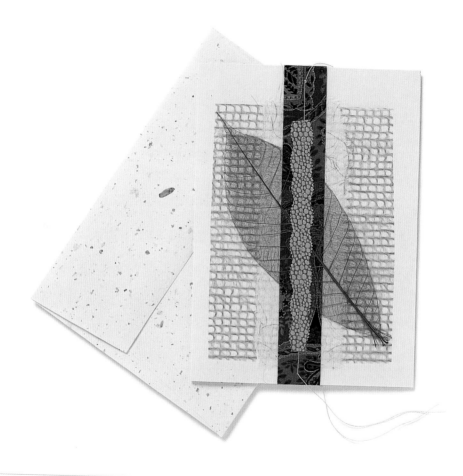

0035   **DESIGN:** Peggy Pelletier

0036-0038   Muse Inspired
DESIGN: Victoria Kens

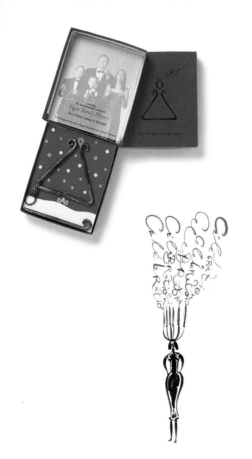

GA GAFIA HHH **h** 12.2002

SMOff

Serious Mode Off

LOL

Laugh Out Loud

\<g\>

grin

0044 | Hecht Design
DESIGN: Studio

0045   UP Creative Design & Advertising
DESIGN: Jenny Pai

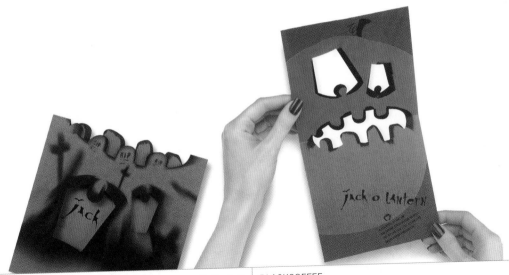

0046

BLACKCOFFEE
DESIGN: Mark Gallagher, Laura Savard

May your
vowels
be airy
and light
And may
all your
consonants
be right.

0051 Tracy Design
DESIGN: Rachel Karaca, Sarah Bray

swedish
meatballs

chestnut
stuffing

0052 | That's Nice LLC
DESIGN: Erica Heitman

SCENTED-GREETING

TANNENBAUM

WHO
WHAT
WHERE
WHEN
WHY

HAPPY
BELATED
BIRTH
DAY

TWAS 234 NIGHTS BEFORE CHRISTMAS

and all through the house, not much was going on because it was a Saturday. Mrs. while folding the laundry, came across her old kerchief and wondered when she'd ever seen anything stupid like that again while Pa took off his cap, unbuttoned his top pants button, and settled in to nap on the couch while watching Battle of the Network Stars. A stocking hung by the chimney, but that was Mrs.' and a result of the kids spending last night at Grandma's.

ABSOLUTELY NO ONE,
NOT THE MAN WHO INVENTED
the limousine or the garage, not the man who came up with the penguin and the porpoise or the dishwasher in their cage, not the man who created the grill, the intimate edition, the high low or watchword expanding treasures, not even the man responsible for the undefeated cinematic treatments of our cheese, explosions and ball. Earnest reality deserves any greater admiration than you do Dad.

HE KNOWS WHEN YOU ARE SLEEPING

And apparently he also knows when you're awake. Which begs the question, "Where ya hiding the surveillance cameras fat man?" And while we're asking questions, just what are the standards for deciding who's naughty and nice anyway? It's totally arbitrary, isn't it? Besides, what's naughty in Charlotte is neighborly behavior in Van Nuys. So where's the manual? Where's the government approved, three-ring binder of guidelines? Santa?

ABSOLUTELY NO MOM,
NOT THE ONE WHO TIED THE FIRST
double knot, first groomed her nails when at first sneered at close, not the Mom who made the best hair-memos, her eight crowns for volcano, nor the Mom who preferred Teglican Linguistics ("You want me to separate you two? Is that what you want? You want to be separated?"), and no, not even the Mom who later smothered her life, career and knows bathroom privacy deserves greater admiration than you do.

0062   plus design inc.
DESIGN: Anita Meyer

0063   **DESIGN:** Swirly Designs by Lianne & Paul

0064   Towers Perrin
     DESIGN: Media Consultants

0065   ARTiculation Group
     DESIGN: Joseph Chan, James Ayotte

0066   Tom Fowler, Inc.
     DESIGN: Brien O'Reilly

0067	EM Press **DESIGN:** Elias Roustom	0069	**DESIGN:** Finished Art, Inc. (Barbara Dorn, Luis Fernandez, Kannex Funk, Li-Kim Goh, Mary Jane Hasek, David Lawson, Rachele Mock, Sutti Sahunalu, Linda Stuart)
0068	Julia Tam Design **DESIGN:** Julia Chong Tam	0070	Popcorn Initiative **DESIGN:** Chris Jones, Roger Wood

0075 Asher Studio
DESIGN: Russ Chilcoat, Gretchen Wilis

0076   Riordan Design
DESIGN: Shirley Riordon, Amy Montgomery

0081

ZGraphics, Ltd.
DESIGN: Kris Martinez Farrell

DON WE NOW OUR GAY APPAREL

02 › 03

Sorry I'm late!
Sorry I'm late!
Sorry I'm late!
Sorry I'm late!
Sorry I'm late!
Sorry I'm late!
Sorry I'm late!
Sorry I'm late!

FOR MY BETTER 1/2

0090-0091 **DESIGN:** Peggy Pelletier

0092   **DESIGN:** Scott Baldwin

0093   John Evans Design
        DESIGN: John Evans

0094   Miro Design
        DESIGN: Judy Glenzer

0095   John Evans Design
        DESIGN: John Evans

0096   Fiddlesticks Press
DESIGN: Lynn Amft

0097   **DESIGN:** Sayre Gaydos

0098   **DESIGN:** Little Smiles Co.

0099   Bob's Your Uncle
DESIGN: Martin Yeeles

0100   KBDA
DESIGN: Jamie Diersing

0101 | BLANK, Inc.
DESIGN: Danielle Willis

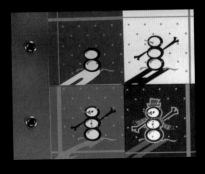

It was always snowing at Christmas. When we rode the daft and happy hills bareback, it snowed and it snowed. Our snow was not only shaken from whitewash buckets down the sky, it swam and drifted out of the arms and hands and bodies of the trees; snow grew overnight on the roofs of the houses, minutely white-iced the walls and settled on the chilly glinting hill, like a thunderstorm of white, torn Christmas cards. And the silent one-clouded heavens drifted on to the sea.

0106	Sayles Graphic Design **DESIGN:** John Sayles, Som Inthalangsy	0108	Choplogic **DESIGN:** Walter McCord
0107	graphische formgebung **DESIGN:** Herbert Rohsiepe	0109	Rick Johnson & Company **DESIGN:** Tim McGrath

0110 | Blue Inc.
DESIGN: Nina Max Daly

| 0111 | Tong Design Graphic Studio
DESIGN: Tong Wai Hang | 0113 | Rome & Gold Creative
DESIGN: Lorenzo Romero |
| 0112 | UP Creative Design & Advertising Co.
DESIGN: Peter Lee | 0114 | Nassar Design
DESIGN: Margarita Encomienda, Nelida Nassar |

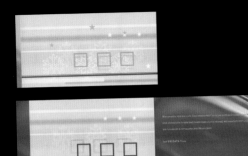

0119   **DESIGN:** Ann Conneman

WHOOPS
A
DAISY

YOU MAY
NOW
KISS
THE BRIDE

SINCE
SLICED
BREAD

SUPER
CALI
FRAGILISTIC
EXPIALI
DOCIOUS!

| 0120 | Bob's Your Uncle
DESIGN: Martin Yeeles | 0122 | Bob's Your Uncle
DESIGN: Martin Yeeles |
| 0121 | Bob's Your Uncle
DESIGN: Martin Yeeles | 0123 | Bob's Your Uncle
DESIGN: Martin Yeeles |

0124	CC Graphic Design **DESIGN:** Carolyn Crowley	0126	hagopian ink **DESIGN:** Christina Hagopian
0125	Brookline Street Design, Ltd. **DESIGN:** Heather Snyder Quinn	0127	Red Design **DESIGN:** Red Design

CRE·A·TIV·I·TEA

CRE·A·TIV·I·TEA

Heavy-hitting creativity with a
gentle herbal trust infusion.

Happy Holidays!
from SK Visual

graphic design
www.skvisual.com   212.956.0071

Product of The Republic of Tea

have a **warm** and wonderful
HOLIDAY SEASON!

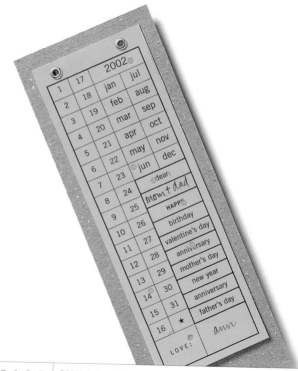

0129   **DESIGN:** Ann Connemann

☐ naughty   ☐ nice

From our often boisterous but always happy household to yours,
best wishes for an enjoyable holiday practiced within the most joyous
traditions of the religious persuasion of your choice.

0138 | Sudduth Design Co.
DESIGN: Toby Sudduth

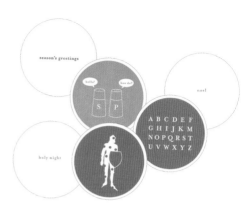

THIS HOLIDAY SEASON MAY EVERYTHING SPELL JOY AND HAPPINESS

WITH LOVE FROM JOYCE ELIASON

GREETINGS

open to play

THIS SEA

0143 Design Dairy
DESIGN: H. Locascio

A loving hug
A kiss or two
A ton of friends (and family too)
A hint of laughter
A dash of fun
A splash of good cheer...

Happy Holidays
from Splash Interactive

Recipe for Holiday Spirits

splash
[interactive]

Enjoy!

0144   Splash Interactive
DESIGN: Ivy Wong

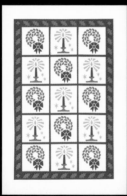

| 0145 | Indian Hill Press
DESIGN: Daniel A. Waters | 0147 | Indian Hill Press
DESIGN: Daniel A. Waters |
| 0146 | Indian Hill Press
DESIGN: Daniel A. Waters | 0148 | Indian Hill Press
DESIGN: Daniel A. Waters |

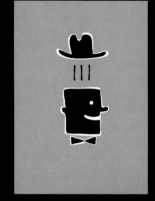

0153   Metzler & Associes
DESIGN: A. Pavion

0154 | Kolegram Design
DESIGN: Jean-Francois Plante

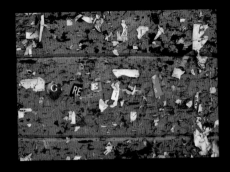

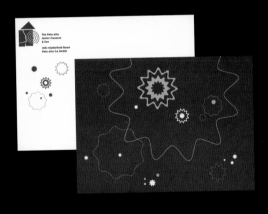

| 0159 | Miro Design
DESIGN: Judy Glenzer | 0161 | Miro Design
DESIGN: Judy Glenzer |
| 0160 | Miro Design
DESIGN: Judy Glenzer | 0162 | Miro Design
DESIGN: Judy Glenzer |

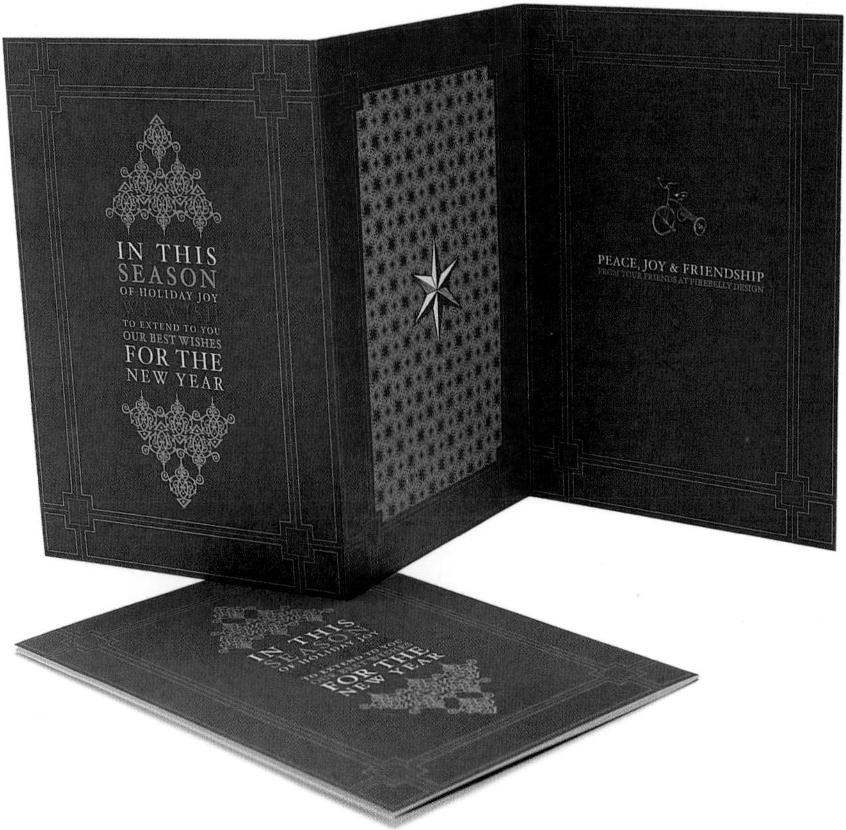
IN THIS
SEASON
OF HOLIDAY JOY
WE WISH
TO EXTEND TO YOU
OUR BEST WISHES
FOR THE
NEW YEAR
PEACE, JOY & FRIENDSHIP
FROM YOUR FRIENDS AT FIREBELLY DESIGN

0163 Firebelly Design
DESIGN: Mikel Rosenthal

OUR BUNDLE OF CHRISTMAS JOY

WINTER

0164 Brookline Street Design, Ltd.
DESIGN: Heather Snyder Quinn

SUGAR
AND SPICE
AND ALL THAT'S
NICE

SLUGS
AND SNAILS
AND PUPPY DOGS'
TAILS

AND
MANY
MORE

21
AGAIN

QVINCY JONES

MUSIC PUBLISHING

Make

a

wish

is good...

...but two is better!

Let's get together!

0173   Wilson Harvey
DESIGN: Wai Lau

0174   Riordon Design
        DESIGN: Amy Montgomery

| 0175 | **DESIGN:** Sayre Gaydos | 0177 | **DESIGN:** Sayre Gaydos |
| 0176 | **DESIGN:** Sayre Gaydos | 0178 | **DESIGN:** Sayre Gaydos |

0179	Indian Hill Press **DESIGN:** Daniel A. Waters	0181	Indian Hill Press **DESIGN:** Daniel A. Waters
0180	W. C. Burgard Illustration **DESIGN:** W. C. Burgard	0182	Smudge Ink **DESIGN:** Kate Saliba

0183   ARTiculation Group
DESIGN: Joseph Chan, Wilson Lam, Helen Ng, Karin Fukuzawa

0184   ZGraphics, Ltd.
       DESIGN: Kris Martinez Farrell

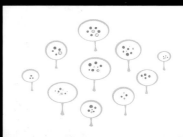

| 0185 | Megan Webber Design
DESIGN: Megan Webber | 0187 | Simon Does
DESIGN: Karen Simon |

MERRY CHRISTMAS

And A HAPPY
NEW
YEAR. JOYeuX
NOëL
et BONNE!
ANnéE!
ZALig KERSTFEEST
En g.LuKKig NieuwJAAR

THERE IS NO JOY

ALEX, I'LL TAKE
LOVE
FOR A HUNDRED

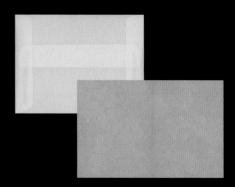

| 0189 | Gervais
DESIGN: Francois Gervais | 0191 | Design Dairy
DESIGN: Joyce Eliason |
| 0190 | **DESIGN:** Dairy | 0192 | **DESIGN:** Smudge Ink |

0197 **DESIGN:** Form Funf Bremen

0198   **DESIGN:** John Kallio Graphic Design

0199   John Evans Design
      DESIGN: John Evans

0200   Wallace Church
      DESIGN: Stan Church

0201   Riordon Design
      DESIGN: Tim Warnock

0206 | Gervais/Citron Vert
DESIGN: Francois Gervais

0207 | Yee Design
DESIGN: Danny Yee, Sue Yee

0212	Indian Hill Press **DESIGN:** Daniel A. Waters	0214	Indian Hill Press **DESIGN:** Daniel A. Waters
0213	Indian Hill Press **DESIGN:** Daniel A. Waters	0215	Indian Hill Press **DESIGN:** Daniel A. Waters

0216

McCullough Creative Group, Inc.
DESIGN: McCullough Creative Team

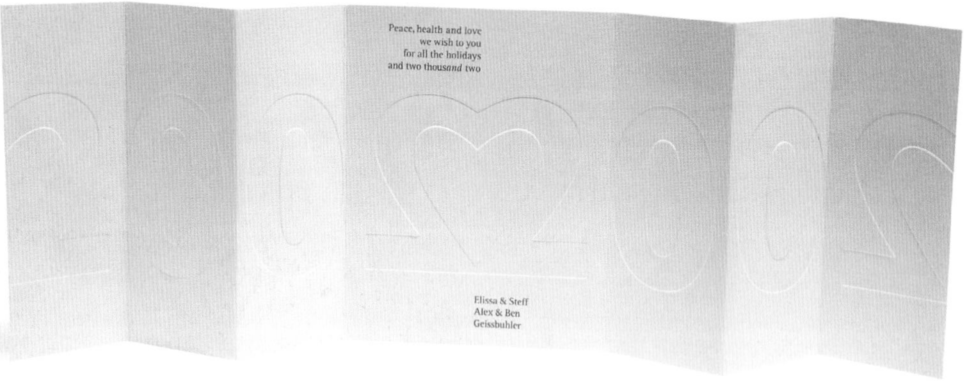

Peace, health and love
we wish to you
for all the holidays
and two thousand two

Elissa & Steff
Alex & Ben
Geissbuhler

0217 Chermayeff & Geismar, Inc.
DESIGN: Steff Geissbuhler

HAPPY**MAY**DAY!

SINCE ANCIENT TIMES, MAY FIRST HAS BEEN A DAY FOR OUTDOOR FESTIVALS. THE ENGLISH HAVE OBSERVED MAY DAY SINCE MEDIEVAL TIMES. PEOPLE WOULD GO INTO THE FOREST TO GATHER FLOWERS AND BRANCHES OF TREES TO DECORATE THEIR HOMES. A MAY QUEEN WAS CROWNED TO REIGN OVER THE GAMES AND DANCING AROUND A STREAMER-LADEN MAY POLE. *But streamer-laden poles aside, what's the happs?*

ELECTION**DAY**AGAIN?

EVERY FOUR YEARS, ON THE TUESDAY AFTER THE FIRST MONDAY IN OCTOBER, REGISTERED VOTERS IN THE UNITED STATES VOTE FOR PRESIDENTIAL ELECTORS. COLLECTIVELY, THESE ELECTORS FORM THE ELECTORAL COLLEGE. THESE ELECTORS MEET ON THE FIRST TUESDAY AFTER THE SECOND WEDNESDAY IN DECEMBER TO ELECT THE PRESIDENT AND VICE-PRESIDENT. ALMOST NO ONE UNDERSTANDS THIS, *but it's a good excuse to see if you do and say hello.*

| 0218 | Bob's Your Uncle
DESIGN: Martin Yeeles | 0220 | **DESIGN:** Dairy |
| 0219 | **DESIGN:** Dairy | 0221 | Bob's Your Uncle
DESIGN: Martin Yeeles |

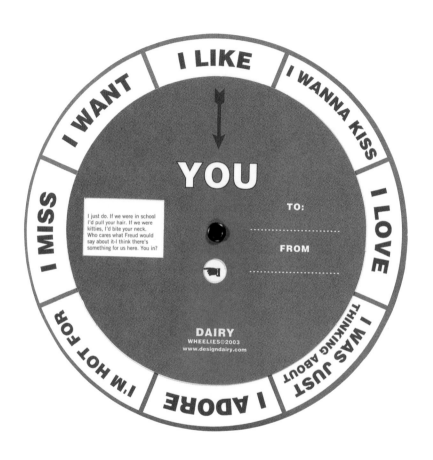

0222

DESIGN: Dairy

DESIGN: Dairy

Happy Holidays

| 0224 | **DESIGN:** Sayre Gaydos | 0226 | **DESIGN:** Sayre Gaydos |
| 0225 | **DESIGN:** Sayre Gaydos | 0227 | **DESIGN:** Sayre Gaydos |

Wishing you a year of
eggcitement, abundance and wealth

eggcreatives.

0228 | Egg Creatives
DESIGN: Kevin Lee

0229   energy energy design
DESIGN: Jeanette Aramburu

COOCHY
COOCHY
COO!

BON VOYAGE

GET
WELL
AT ONCE

OLD
NEW
BORROWED
BLUE

Bob's Your Uncle
DESIGN: Martin Yeeles

Bob's Your Uncle
DESIGN: Martin Yeeles

0236

0237

Bob's Your Uncle
DESIGN: Martin Yeeles

Bob's Your Uncle
DESIGN: Martin Yeeles

0238 | Mindwalk Design Group, Inc.
DESIGN: Michael Huggins

0239　Nassar Design
DESIGN: Margarita Encomienda, Nelida Nassar

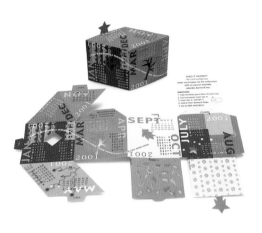

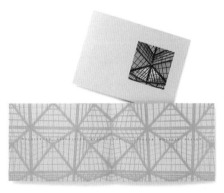

0240	Artistic Announcements **DESIGN:** K. E. Roehr	0242	Anvil Graphic Design, Inc. **DESIGN:** Gary Wong, Cathy Chin
0241	Nassar Design **DESIGN:** Margarita Encomienda, Nelida Nassar	0243	And Partners **DESIGN:** David Schimmel

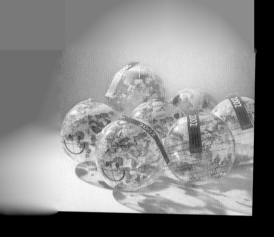

He wore blue suede shoes, shook his pelvis, and was known by the other elves as Elf-vis

Merry Mix-Mess

McCullough Creative Group, Inc.
DESIGN: Greg Dietzenbach

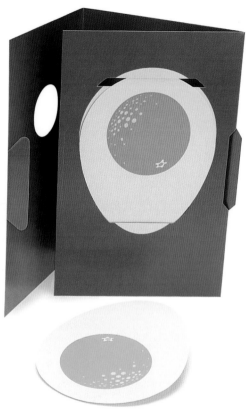

0249 Egg Creatives
DESIGN: Lim Choon Pin

0250   Timespin
DESIGN: Tino Schmidt

0251   **DESIGN:** Stacey Bakaj

0252   Dig Design
DESIGN: Amy Decker

0253   Riordon Design
DESIGN: Tim Warnock

| 0254 | IC Company In-house
DESIGN: Vibeke Nodskov | 0256 | **DESIGN:** Kristina E. Kim |
| 0255 | **DESIGN:** Kristina E. Kim | 0257 | **DESIGN:** Kristina E. Kim |

0258 | Brookline Street Design, Ltd.
DESIGN: Heather Snyder Quinn

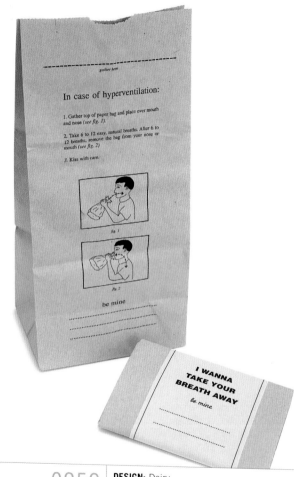

In case of hyperventilation:

1. Gather top of paper bag and place over mouth and nose *(see fig. 1)*.

2. Take 6 to 12 easy, natural breaths. After 6 to 12 breaths, remove the bag from your nose or mouth *(see fig. 2)*

3. Kiss with care.

fig. 1

fig. 2

be mine

I WANNA
TAKE YOUR
BREATH AWAY
be mine

0259   **DESIGN:** Dairy

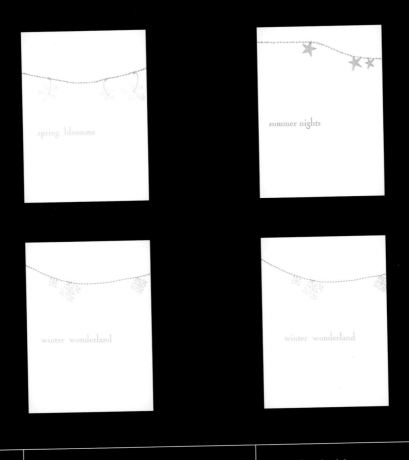

0260   **DESIGN:** Smudge Ink

0261   **DESIGN:** Smudge Ink

0262   **DESIGN:** Smudge Ink

0263   **DESIGN:** Smudge Ink

0264	Group 55 Marketing **DESIGN:** Jeannette Gutierrez	0266	John Kneapler Design **DESIGN:** Holly Buckley, John Kneapler
0265	Group 55 Marketing **DESIGN:** Jeannette Gutierrez	0267	Sonsoles Llorens Design **DESIGN:** Sonsoles Llorens

0268   Riordon Design
DESIGN: Amy Montgomery, Sharon Pece

0269

Michael Osborne Design
DESIGN: Paul Kagiwada, Michelle Regen Bogen

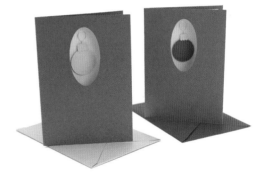

Take the first right, then next left just after the roundabout, carry on, it should be coming up on your left. That's it. Almost there. Now go straight up to the top. Take the small opening and go all the way down. Stand up and go through to the next room. Find stocking.

0274	Roundel	0276	McGINTY
	DESIGN: Paul Ingle		**DESIGN:** Matt Rue, Kyle Russell
0275	**DESIGN:** M. J. Bronstein	0277	Vestigio
			DESIGN: Emanuel Barbosa

0278 Design Dairy
DESIGN: H. Locascio

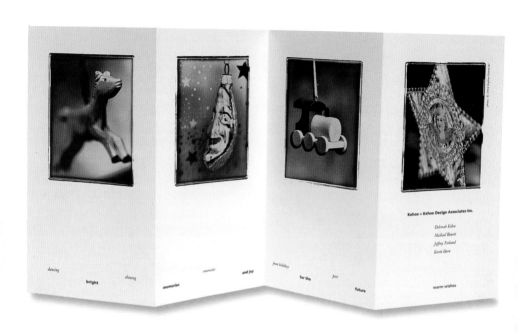

dancing   *shining*

bright

(memories)   **and joy**

memories

from holidays   *past*

for the

future

Kehoe + Kehoe Design Associates Inc.

Deborah Kehoe
Michael Benoit
Jeffrey Forland
Korin Hern

warm wishes

0279   Kehoe & Kehoe Design Associates
DESIGN: Deborah Kehoe

Thank you for the beautiful _____.
Not only will it make an excellent addition
to our _____, but it makes us
_____ every time we look at it. You
were so _____ to think of us.

HAPPY**FAT**TUESDAY!

FAT TUESDAY IS MARDI GRAS, THE FESTIVAL NEW ORLEANS,
LOUISIANA, IS FAMOUS FOR. THE ANNUAL FESTIVITIES
START ON JANUARY 6, WHEN THE THREE KINGS ARE SUPPOSED
TO HAVE VISITED THE CHRIST CHILD, AND BUILD TO A
CLIMAX ON FAT TUESDAY, WHICH ALWAYS OCCURS ON THE DAY
BEFORE ASH WEDNESDAY. *So happy tuesday, and
whenever you get this, happy that day, too.*

I love you more than_____ :

☐ mashed potatoes
☐ sleep
☐ champagne
☐ all of the above

HAPPY**FLAG** DAY!

FLAG DAY, THE ANNIVERSARY OF THE FLAG RESOLUTION OF 1777,
WAS OFFICIALLY ESTABLISHED BY PRESIDENT WILSON ON MAY 30TH,
1916. IT WASN'T UNTIL 1949, THAT PRESIDENT TRUMAN SIGNED AN
ACT OF CONGRESS DESIGNATING JUNE 14TH OF EACH YEAR AS
NATIONAL FLAG DAY. *That said, how's it hanging?*

| 0280 | **DESIGN:** Dairy | 0282 | **DESIGN:** Dairy |
| 0281 | **DESIGN:** Dairy | 0283 | **DESIGN:** Dairy |

_____,

I was just thinking about_____:

☐ the stock market
☐ current events
☐ the meaning of life
☐ you

I miss _____:

☐ the eighties
☐ puberty
☐ beta
☐ you

FULL NAME: Mud

I'M SORRY

| 0284 | **DESIGN:** Dairy | 0286 | **DESIGN:** Dairy |
| 0285 | **DESIGN:** Dairy | 0287 | **DESIGN:** Dairy |

0292

Hutchinson Associates, Inc.
DESIGN: Jerry Hutchinson

| 0293 | Indian Hill Press
DESIGN: Daniel A. Waters | 0295 | Indian Hill Press
DESIGN: Daniel A. Waters |
| 0294 | Indian Hill Press
DESIGN: Daniel A. Waters | 0296 | Indian Hill Press
DESIGN: Daniel A. Waters |

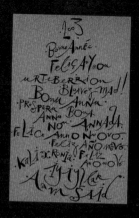

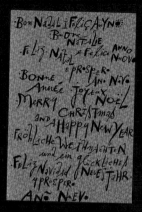

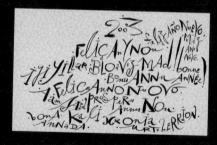

0297	Gervais	0299	Gervais
	DESIGN: Francois Gervais		**DESIGN:** Francois Gervais
0298	Gervais	0300	Gervais
	DESIGN: Francois Gervais		**DESIGN:** Francois Gervais

0301   hagopian ink
        DESIGN: Christina Hagopian

0302-0304 | **DESIGN:** Kristina E. Kim

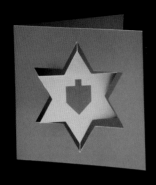

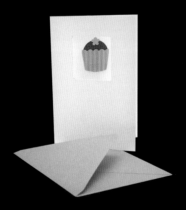

SO YOUR ODOMETER
JUST CLICKED OVER THE OTHER DAY

You made it once more around the sun. You're another year closer to taking part in organized Bingo. You're well on your way to relaxe-fastened walking shoes, shuffleboard, and a community in Central Florida where everyone drives around in golf carts but, for some reason, never really plays golf. But until then, Happy Birthday. And, oh yeah, keep an eye out for "The Letter" from the AARP.

SOME QUESTIONS
THAT HAVE NOT ONCE BEEN UTTERED:

Dare, the guys and I are gonna go paint posters, wanna come? Fitness anyone? You think that "Hang in There" kitten poster is what saved his life? Meet me for drinks at the tall booth please? Who are mums? Could I get "Papa Forever Local 507" stitched in a pillow please? Dude, check out that elementary school cafeteria worker—has milk done that body good or what?

FOR ONE DAY
INSIST THAT EVERYONE GREET YOU

with the phrase, "Aye Aye Cap'n." Reduce your vocabulary to two words: 'arrr' and 'harrar.' Answer the phone in the voice of a professional wrestler. Stay up late and order two dozen porcelain curling monkeys from the home shopping channel. Why? Because you can. It's your birthday. And you'll have to wait another 365 days before you're licensed to behave with such reckless abandon again.

OPPORTUNITY
IS NOT JUST KNOCKING

it's busting through the back door and snapping you with a wet towel. Youir graduate, these doors are gonna swing wide. Perhaps you'll be a driftwood artist. Or a hostage negotiator. An aluminum siding salesman. Or a respected Appalachian linguistics export maybe. You could even be a synchronized swimmer that remembers that routine. Mama didn't raise no underachievers!

IF YOU HAD KETCHUP
PACKETS IN YOUR GLOVE BOX

I'd have french fries on my floorboard. If you had an "I'm with Stupid" t-shirt, I'd have a gun wearing hat. If you shouted "Yahtzee" at dinner, I'd shout "Bingo." If you produced a television show called "America's Funniest Animal Attacks," I'd suddenly get mauled by a panda. What I'm trying to get at here is that somehow, someway, you and I just seem to be made for each other.

THE DAY YOU
SAID YES WAS NOT

the day he got on a knee and asked you. It was not the day you determined what side of the bed you prefer. And it was not the day you decided you were perfectly okay with the trembling face that he danced like a six-year-old trying to stay on the head of his shadow. No, the day you honestly, truly said yes was the day you put his name down in the "Who to Notify in Case of Emergency" section.

WHY? WHY? WHY?
WHY IS THE SKY BLUE? WHY DOES

poop smell? Why does Billy have two dads? Why does Uncle Larry's house have wheels? Why can't Mr. Fergie and Mr. Electrical Socket be friends? Why isn't Johnnyslittlecheeseorwhatsit my aunt too? Congratulations Mom and Dad. Your lives are about to be filled with more peculiar question than a congressional hearing. But whatever you get asked don't ever forget the one right answer. Because I said so, that's why.

DON'T GET YOUR MEAT
WHERE YOU GET YOUR BREAD

is an axiom I usually adhere to. However, I'm starting to think I might have to amend it just this once. Besides, who couldn't you get your meat and bread at the same place? I mean, else how stupidly inefficient is that? So don't be too surprised if sometime in the next few days, I walk up to you in the hallway, shoot you the double barreled fingers and say, "What is happenin' hotstuff?"

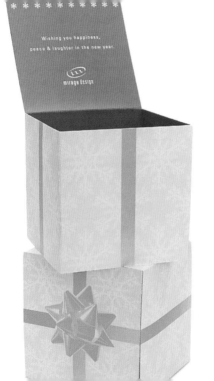

Wishing you happiness,
peace & laughter in the new year.

mirage design

| 0318 | Indian Hill Press
DESIGN: Daniel A. Waters | 0320 | Indian Hill Press
DESIGN: Daniel A. Waters |
| 0319 | John Evans Design
DESIGN: John Evans | 0321 | Indian Hill Press
DESIGN: Daniel A. Waters |

IN ONE HOUR
I CAN MAKE 20 3-MINUTE EGGS

I'm an honest tax payer and a responsible consumer.
I've got ketchup packets in my glove compartment, and I
have to jiggle the handle to make my toilet stop running.
By all this I just mean to say that I'm a reasonably normal
person with a reasonably normal life. That is, except for the
increasingly obvious fact that I have a raging crush on you.

IF YOU LEAVE ME

can i come too?

baby

smile

Never knock on Death's door: ring the bell and run away! Death really hates that!

—Matt Frewer
as Dr. Mike Stratford
in Doctor, Doctor

Happy Holidays from Steve Fleshman

Ring in the New

Ring out the Old

www.dr-2.com

Concept, copy, design and photography by Steven D. Fleshman ©2002 Steven D. Fleshman

0326 DR2
DESIGN: Steven D. Fleshman

MERRY CHRISTMAS AND A HAPPY NEW YORK

M M
O

HAPPY MOTHER'S DAY

GET BETTER SOON

2 0

One

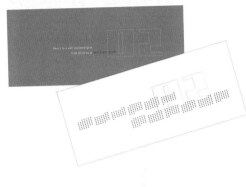

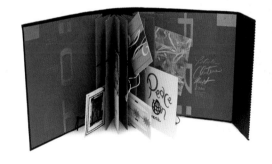

CELEBRATE

your family

0343   IE Design
DESIGN: Marcie Carson, Richard Haynie

0348	Refinery Design Company **DESIGN:** Julie Schmalz	0350	After Hours Creative **DESIGN:** After Hours Creative
0349	Mirage Design **DESIGN:** Lynette Allaire	0351	Design Dairy **DESIGN:** H. Locassio

0352-0354   **DESIGN:** John Cameron

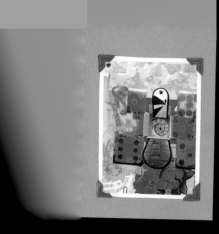

Muse Inspired
DESIGN: Victoria Kens

Kevin Akers Design & Imagery

Muse Inspired
DESIGN: Victoria Kens

DESIGN: Michael Osborne Design

0359-0360   **DESIGN:** Peggy Pelletier

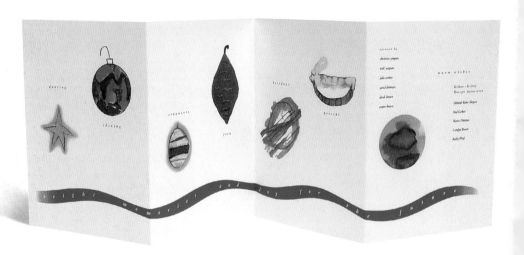

0361   Kehoe & Kehoe Design Associates
       DESIGN: Deborah Kehoe

'Twas the night before Christm. . .

%*#@$!

I procrastinated (again)!
Hope you had
a warm and
wonderful holiday.

Have a happy
New Year!

TAKE ONE EVERY DAY

HAPPY
BIRTHDAY

0370 Egg Creatives
DESIGN: Jason Chen

0371-0375

Fiddlesticks Press
DESIGN: Lynne Amft

e m m a

SEASONED ARMADILLO

KISS ○ ○ ○ ○
LOVE ○ ○ ○ ○
HUG ○ ○ ○ ○
BE ○ ○ ○ ○

HAPPY VALENTINE'S DAY

| 0376 | Brookline Street Design, Ltd.
DESIGN: Heather Snyder Quinn | 0378 | Megan Webber Design
DESIGN: Wendy Carnegie, Julie Savakis |
| 0377 | Greta Berger
DESIGN: Greta Berger | 0379 | Towers Perrin
DESIGN: Lavonne Czech |

0380   Gervais/Citron Vert
DESIGN: Francois Gervais

0381   Bandujo, Donker & Brothers
DESIGN: Laura Astuto, Anne Dennis

0382   W. C. Burgard Illustration
DESIGN: W. C. Burgard

0383   Gervais
DESIGN: Francois Gervais

HAPPYARBORDAY!

ARBOR DAY IS A NATIONALLY CELEBRATED OBSERVANCE THAT ENCOURAGES TREE PLANTING AND TREE CARE. FOUNDED BY J. STERLING MORTON IN NEBRASKA IN 1872, NATIONAL ARBOR DAY IS CELEBRATED EACH YEAR ON THE LAST FRIDAY IN APRIL, SO YES, HAPPY ARBOR DAY, *but really I just wanted to say hiya.*

HAPPYBOXINGDAY!

THE DAY AFTER CHRISTMAS, THE FEAST OF ST. STEPHEN IS BETTER KNOWN AS BOXING DAY. THE TERM MAY COME FROM THE OPENING OF CHURCH POOR BOXES THAT DAY; OR MAYBE FROM THE BOXES WITH WHICH APPRENTICES COLLECTED MONEY AT THE DOORS OF THEIR MASTERS' CLIENTS, e... *way, i was just wondering how you were...*

HAPPYGROUNDHOGDAY!

FEBRUARY 2 IS GROUNDHOG DAY, THE DAY THAT THE GROUNDHOG COMES OUT OF HIS HOLE AFTER WINTER HIBERNATION TO LOOK FOR HIS SHADOW. BY SEEING IT, HE FORETELLS SIX MORE WEEKS OF BAD WHETHER AND GOES BACK INTO HIS HOLE. IF HE DOESN'T, HE STAYS OUT. INDICATING THAT SPRING IS NEAR. STATISTICAL EVIDENCE DOES NOT SUPPORT THIS TRADITION, *but I thought it a really fine reason to write and say i was thinking about you.*

0384-0386

DESIGN: Dairy

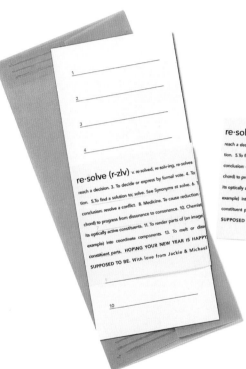

re·solve (r-zlv) v. re-solved, re-solv-ing, re-solves v. tr. 1. To make a firm decision about. 2. To cause (a person) to reach a decision. 3. To decide or express by formal vote. 4. To change or convert: My resentment resolved itself into resignation. 5. To find a solution to; solve. See Synonyms at solve. 6. To remove or dispel (doubts). 7. To bring to a usually successful conclusion: resolve a conflict. 8. Medicine. To cause reduction of (an inflammation, for example). 9. Music. To cause (a tone or chord) to progress from dissonance to consonance. 10. Chemistry. To separate (an optically inactive compound or mixture) into its optically active constituents. 11. To render parts of (an image) visible and distinct. 12. Mathematics. To separate (a vector, for example) into coordinate components. 13. To melt or dissolve (something). 14. Archaic. To separate (something) into constituent parts. **HOPING YOUR NEW YEAR IS HAPPY, RESOLUTE, AND THAT EVERYTHING IS WHERE IT'S SUPPOSED TO BE.** With love from JACKIE & MIRO.

CAPE COD

In the lower arm extension of Massachusetts,
the shoulder of at Buzzards Bay,
the elbow at sharp bend of Cape Wellfleet,
the wrist at Truro,
and the sandy fist at Provincetown.

—Henry David Thoreau

cape cod

CAPE COD

CAPE COD

CAPE COD

FALMOUTH SANDWICH BOURNE MASHPEE
BARNSTABLE HYANNIS YARMOUTH DENNIS
BREWSTER HARWICH CHATHAM ORLEANS
EASTHAM WELLFLEET TRURO PROVINCETOWN
NANTUCKET AND MARTHA'S VINEYARD

0392-0396   hagopian ink
DESIGN: Christina Hagopian

0397	Bah! Design	0399	**DESIGN:** Dairy
	DESIGN: Scott Herron	0400	**DESIGN:** Martin Lemelman Illustration
0398	Gulla Design		
	DESIGN: Steve Gulla		

Light, seeking light doth light of light beguile....
William Shakespeare (1564–1616)

Peace
The Stubbins Associates Inc.

0405   Nassar Design
DESIGN: Margarita Encomienda, Nelida Nassar

0406 John Kneapler Design
DESIGN: Colleen Shea

2 0 0 3

0407   d/g brussels
DESIGN: Sally Orr

ETHAN McGREGOR RAWLINS
9 21 02

ANNOUNCEMENTS

CREATED with
LOVE

CARRIED with

HOPE and

WELCOMED with

JOY

Elizabeth Grace
JAKUBEK CRAWFORD

0409

daughter of
ALAN JAKUBEK and CAROLINE CRAWFORD
was welcomed into the world
on Tuesday, March 25th, 2003

A baby is God's opinion that life should go on.
—Carl Sandburg

0408 Kehoe & Kehoe Design Associates
DESIGN: Deborah Kehoe

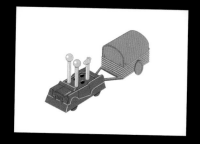

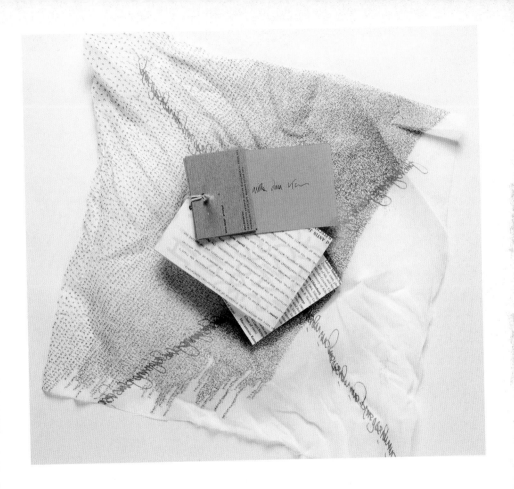

0417
plus design, inc.
DESIGN: Anita Meyer, Karin Fickett, Dina Zaccagnini, Matthew Monk, Jan Baker

0418 Viñas Design
DESIGN: Jaime Viñas

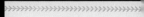

EXCEPT OUR LOCATION.

Edward James
'Ned'

Date: May 5, 2003
Weight: 8 pounds 8 ounces
Disposition: Curious

Katherine and Steve Tagtmeier

egg creatives

3x1

New Address

Marco Beretta

21 de noviembre de 2002 - 1.35 am - 3,120 kg - 48,5 cm

0441 My baby sister...

SIMON

SAYS

Introducing
SIMON FRANKEL
The Proud Parents
TRACY FOX AND PETER FRANKEL

0424 **Hi.**

August 30th, 2002
8:58pm
18 inches long
6 pounds, 7 ounces

10 YEARS OF GRAPHIC DESIGN, OUT THE WINDOW...

We've moved (2 doors down from our old office). The hard part is over, but we could still use your help...
On April 1, 2003, between 11am and 2 pm, come and celebrate our 10th anniversary with us.
Drop by our new studio and join us for an open house and a free lunch.
Please call 321-9804 by March 26 to RSVP.

...AND DOWN THE STREET.

andersonthomas

0427   Hutchinson Associates, Inc.
DESIGN: Jerry Hutchinson

0428   Anderson Thomas Design
DESIGN: Kristi Smith

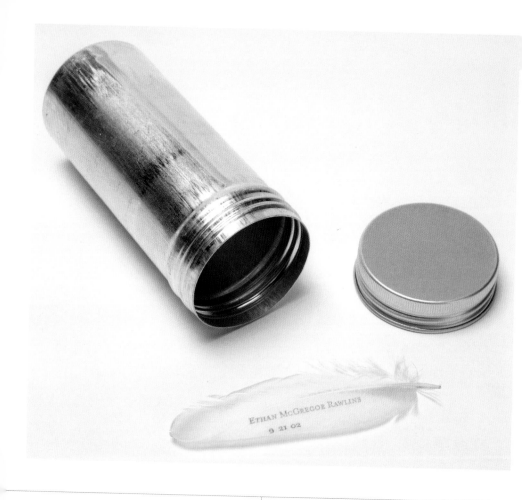

ETHAN McGREGOR RAWLINS
9 21 02

0429   Rick Rawlins/Work
DESIGN: Rick Rawlins

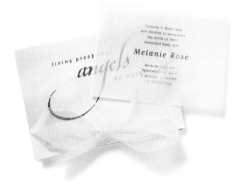

0430	Cave Images, Inc. **DESIGN:** Matt Cave	0432	Porto & Martinez Design Studio **DESIGN:** Bruno Porto
0431	Rule 29 **DESIGN:** Justin Ahrens	0433	Tom Fowler, Inc. **DESIGN:** Brien O'Reilly

IT'S A GIRL
A PINK-BLANKET-TOTING,

Daddy-shoulder-riding, heather-blowing, miniature-porcelain-horse-collecting, Easy-Bake-Oven-cooking, difficult-question-asking, girl-scout-cookie-selling, slumber-party-having, telephone-hogging, bed-room-door-locking, boy-band-loving, absolutely-unacceptable-outfit-wearing, bridal-magazine-reading, just-like-her-Mother little girl.

And that, we're fairly sure, makes us happier than we've ever been.

IT'S A BOY
A BLUE-BLANKET-TOTING,

dirt-eating, tree-climbing, armpit-fart-sound-making, sisters-sand-castle-stomping, swimsuit-tissue-peeking, outside-the-lines-coloring, video-game-playing, back-seat-invisible-line-crossing, pigtail-pulling, bra-strap-snapping, principal's-office-visiting, summer-buzz-cut-having, Dad-when-can-we-go-to-Fenway boy.

And that, we're fairly sure, makes us happier than we've ever been.

Charlie & Kate

54 Middleton Road
London
E8 4BS
t 020 7254 4793
e katie@kashort.freeserve.co.uk

we've moved

0438   Wilson Harvey
DESIGN: Ben Wood

ghislaine, jaime & mia soleil announce the arrival of

saskia luna viñas

born on july 31, 2002
in new york city at 10:33 am

weight: 7.3 lbs. 3.3 kg.
length: 20 in. 50.8 cm.

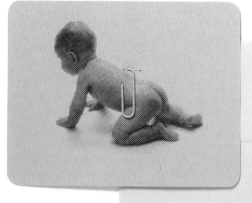

0439

Viñas Design
DESIGN: Jaime Viñas

0440 Knezic/Pavone
      DESIGN: Robinson C. Smith

0441 **DESIGN:** Maren Bottger

0442 Egg Creatives
      DESIGN: Jason Chen

0443 Smudge Ink
      DESIGN: Kate Saliba

0444

Wallace Church, Inc.
DESIGN: Stan Church

n

Nice to meet you,
I'm Cameron

0446 | Cave Images, Inc.
DESIGN: Matt Cave

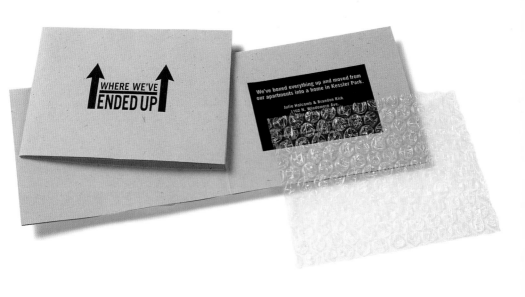

WHERE WE'VE ENDED UP

We've boxed everything up and moved from our apartments into a home in Kessler Park.

Julie Holcomb & Brandon Kirk
1102 N. Windomere Ave.

0447 | Sibley Peteet Design—Dallas
DESIGN: Brandon Kirk

0448   Noon
DESIGN: Cinthia Wen

0449	Alterpop **DESIGN:** Christopher Simmons	0451	BLANK, Inc. **DESIGN:** Danielle Willis
0450	And Partners **DESIGN:** David Schimmel, Sarah Hollowood	0452	Marty Blake Graphic Design **DESIGN:** Marty Blake

0453 Selbert Perkins Design
DESIGN: Avvi Raquel-Santos

0454 | Mirko Ilić Corp
DESIGN: Mirko Ilić, Heath Hingardner

0459   Cave Images
DESIGN: David Edmundson

0460 | KBDA
DESIGN: Jamie Diersing

0461 Suddduth Design Co.
DESIGN: Toby Sudduth

Davian Jolie Schroer

BIRTH
March 25
2002

TIME
8:01am

WEIGHT
4 lbs 12.9 oz

HEIGHT
19.5˝

PARENTS
Sue & Dave

Trent Paulson Schroer

BIRTH
March 25
2002

TIME
8:00am

WEIGHT
5 lbs 14.7 oz

HEIGHT
20.5˝

PARENTS
Sue & Dave

0462   Loudmouth Graphics
DESIGN: David Schroer

Samantha Ming-Ming Roebinson
January Twentieth Two Thousand Two
Seven Pounds Eleven Ounces

JILL & PAUL ROEBINSON

Please visit www.the-roebinsons.com for photos

Chantel and Marc are
moving north.

From the 2nd of August
our new address will be:

103 Aire Row, Wetherby,
West Yorkshire, LS22 7FT
Telephone: 01976 585 62

oliver chase

entered the world on april 2, 2002
weighing 7 pounds and 5 ounces
taylor and annie reader

| 0463 | Roundel **DESIGN:** Paul Ingle | 0465 | 9Spot Monk Design Co. **DESIGN:** Vivian Leung |
| 0464 | Smudge Ink **DESIGN:** Kate Saliba | 0466 | Nassar Design **DESIGN**: Margarita Encomienda, Nelida Nassar |

INVITATIONS

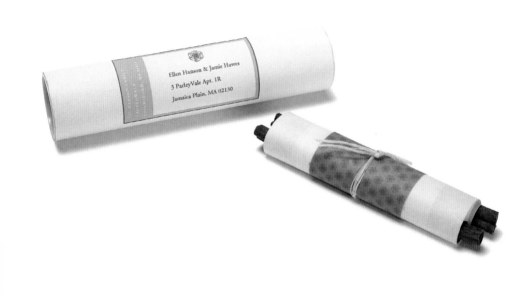

Ellen Hanson & Jamie Hawes
3 ParleyVale Apt. 1R
Jamaica Plain, MA 02130

0467   Brookline Street Design, Ltd.
DESIGN: Heather Snyder Quinn

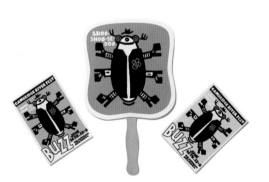

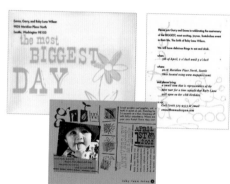

| 0472 | Hans Design
DESIGN: Kristin Miaso | 0474 | Dara Turransky Design
DESIGN: Dara Turransky |
| 0473 | Emma Wilson Design Company
DESIGN: Emma Wilson | 0475 | Brookline Street Design, Ltd.
DESIGN: Heather Snyder Quinn |

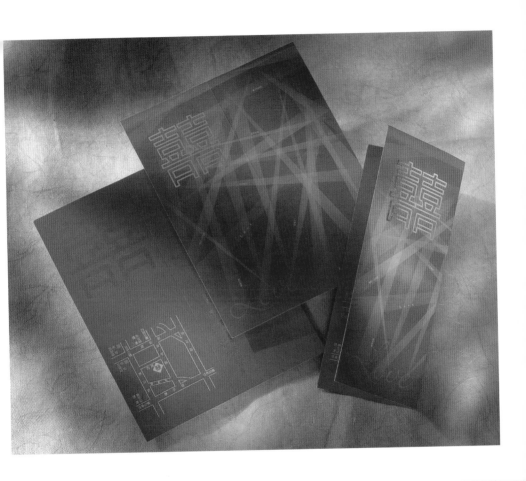

0476   UP Creative Design & Advertising Co.
DESIGN: Javen Lin

0477   Capers Cleveland Design
DESIGN: Jenny Daughters-McLain

0478	Cave Images, Inc. **DESIGN:** Matt Cave	**0480**	KKargl Graphic Design **DESIGN:** Kathleen W. Kargl
0479	inpraxis, raum fur gestaitung **DESIGN:** A. Kranz, C. Schaffner	**0481**	Kristin Cullen **DESIGN:** Kristin Cullen

house*warming

SATURDAY **8.30**PM

23-55 28th street
apartment 8b
astoria 11102
917.982.2183

N/W Astoria Blvd.

JILL & PAUL ROEBINSON
Invite you to the Moon Yuet of
Samantha Ming-Ming

Saturday, March 9, 2002
Seven o'Clock in the evening

Peking Duck House
22 Mott Street
New York

RSVP by February 25
jill@the-roebinsons.com

PLEASE COME TO PAUL CHOPS 30th
BIRTHDAY PARTY

2ND FEBRUARY 2002

FEATURING THE MIGHTY
KENTISH PIE

RSVP: paul@wilsonharvey.co.uk

02.02.02

A BIG DATE FOR THE DIARY

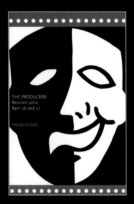

THE PRODUCERS
Reunion 2002
April 26 and 27

PRESENTERS

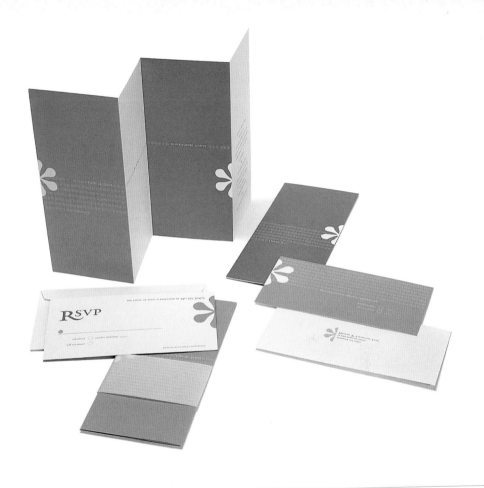

0486 | **DESIGN:** David Salafia, Laura Farr

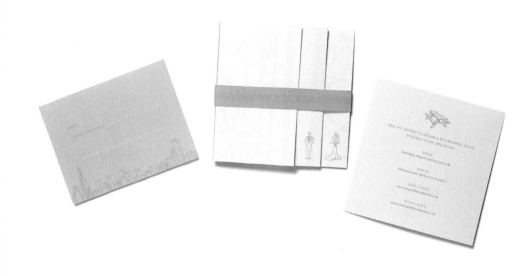

0487   **DESIGN:** Jon McGrath, Jessie Bultema

| 0492 | The Commissary
DESIGN: Alison Charles | 0494 | Gutierrez Design Associates
DESIGN: Jeannette Gutierrez |
| 0493 | Grapevine
DESIGN: Karen Bortolomei | 0495 | Design Dairy
DESIGN: H. Locascio |

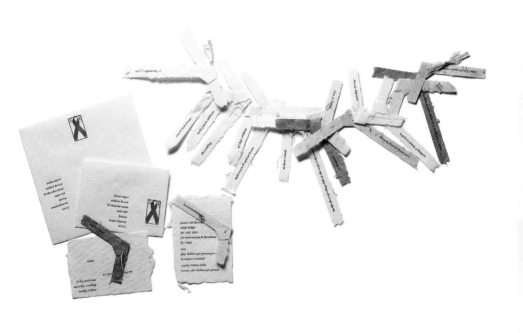

plus design inc.
DESIGN: Anita Meyer, Jan Baker

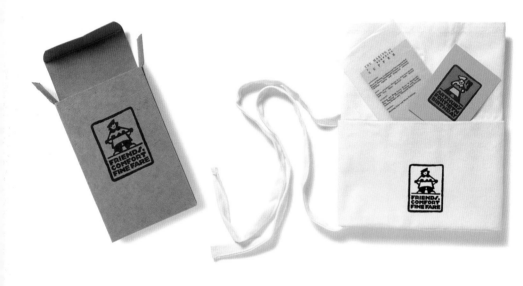

0497

Rick Rawlins/Work
DESIGN: Rick Rawlins

Ryan and Marthea Wilson

0498   **DESIGN:** Carolynn DeCillo Design

0499   Range

      DESIGN: Amy Becker-Jones

0500   Emma Wilson Design Company

      DESIGN: Emma Wilson

0501   BLANK, Inc.

THE HOPE CLINIC
for Women
INVITES YOU TO
enjoy an
AbsenTea

convite | invitation

We've been riding the waves and now
IT'S LUAU TIME

CONSERVE THE DATE

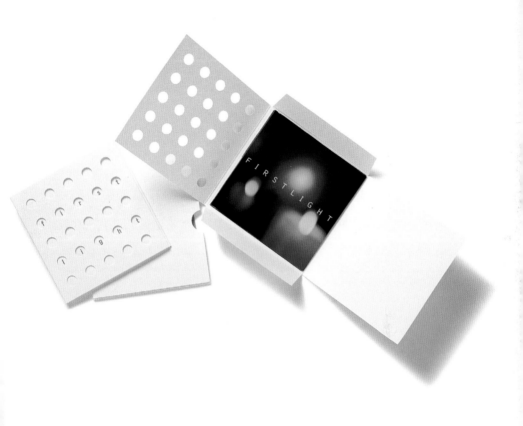

0506 Kendall Ross
DESIGN: David Kendall

0507

Nickelodeon Creative Resources
DESIGN: Erin Blankley

0512	Gunter Advertising **DESIGN:** Sarah Grimm	0514	Goodesign **DESIGN:** Diane Shaw
0513	Emma Wilson Design Company **DESIGN:** Emma Wilson	0515	**DESIGN:** Likovni Studio D.O.O.

0516   Kolegram Design
DESIGN: Annie Tanguay

0517

Insight Design Communications
DESIGN: Lea Carmichael

0518   **DESIGN:** Garet McIntyre

0519   Kevin Akers Design & Imagery
       DESIGN: Kevin Akers

0520   Top Design Studio
       DESIGN: Peleg Top

0521   Egg Creatives
       DESIGN: Jason Chen

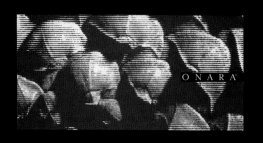

0527   Sayles Graphic Design
DESIGN: John Sayles, Som Inthalangsy

0532   **DESIGN:** Kin Cheung

0533   Greteman Group
       DESIGN: Garrett Fresh

0534   Simply Put Design
       DESIGN: Carrene Tracy

0535   Gee & Chung Design
       DESIGN: Earl Gee, Fani Chung

THINGS TO DO

Saturday Morning Indulgences

The following are some ideas for your visit to Santa Barbara.
April is a busy time so we suggest that you make reservations prior to arrival.

LIZA 310 204 2008 | BILL 310 837 1187
SHARON (Liza's mom) 970 731 4553

0536 Special Modern Design
DESIGN: Karen Barranco

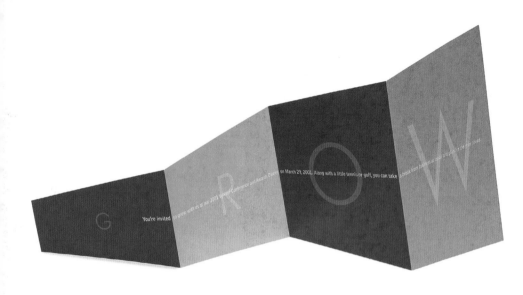

You're invited to grow with us at our 2001 Vendor Conference and Awards Dinner on March 29, 2001. Along with a little tennis or golf, you can take a break from business as usual and join us for the main event.

0537

Design 5
DESIGN: Ron Nikkel

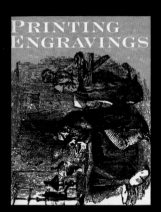

You are cordially
invited to attend the
Tenth Annual
K.I.D.S.S. FOR KIDS
Golf Outing

June 24th 2002

06 28 03 NYC

FIRST ANNUAL
Open
toe Shoe
Party!

one small v👁ice
FOUNDATION

GET INSPIRED!

OPEN HOUSE LUNCHEON

Frasier Papers' design inspiration award show

Sappi's annual report show
printer of the year award

Spicers' annual report show

THURSDAY,
DECEMBER 6TH

R.S.V.P.

SPICERS PAPER

Hutchinson Associates, Inc. **DESIGN:** Jerry Hutchinson	0544	**DESIGN:** Sayre Gaydos
	0545	Emma Wilson Design Company **DESIGN:** Emma Wilson

| 0546 | ZGraphics, Ltd. **DESIGN:** Renee Clark | 0548 | Hams Design **DESIGN:** Renee Kae Szajna |
| 0547 | Michael Courtney Design **DESIGN:** Heidi Fanour, Michael Courtney | 0549 | McCullough Creative Group, Inc. **DESIGN:** Roger Scholbrock |

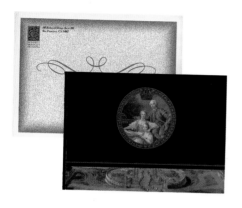

0550	Kevin Akers Design & Imagery **DESIGN:** Kevin Akers	0552	New Idea Design **DESIGN:** Ron Boldt
0551	**DESIGN:** Kristi Norgaard	0553	Emery Vincent Design **DESIGN:** Emery Vincent

0554   Fern Tiger Associates
DESIGN: Fern Tiger

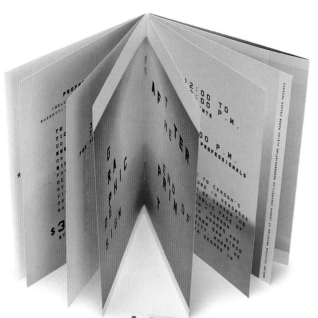

0555   Kolegram Design
DESIGN: Mike Teixeira

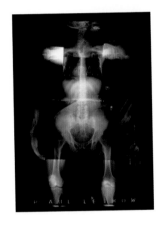

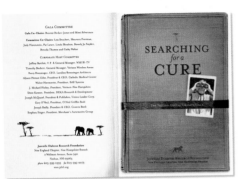

0564	Range **DESIGN:** Steve Richard
0565	Artistic Announcements **DESIGN:** K. E. Roehr
0566	Design Dairy **DESIGN:** H. Locascio
0567	M-Art **DESIGN:** Marty Ittner

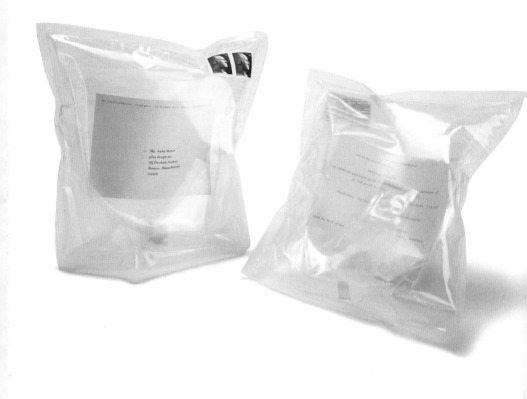

0568 plus design, inc.
DESIGN: Anita Meyer

TOPS
ART
FEST
2003

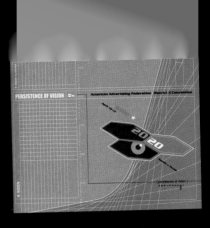

BLANK, Inc.
DESIGN: Christine Dzieciolowski

Michael Courtney Design
DESIGN: Micahel Courtney, Debra Burgess

0571

0572

Bah! Design
DESIGN: Scott Herron, Rob Seale

Uturn Design
DESIGN: Stephanie Zelman

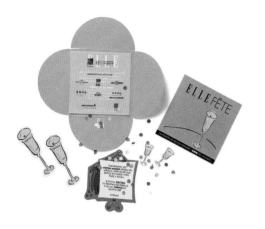

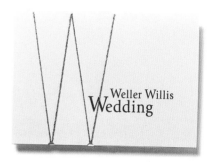

0573	Zappata Disenadores S.C. **DESIGN:** Ibo Angulo	0575	**DESIGN:** Danielle Willis
0574	Innova Ideas & Services **DESIGN:** Jessica Oakland	0576	Refinery Design Company **DESIGN:** Julie Schmalz

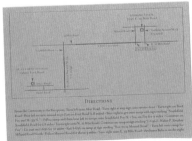

0577 Grapevine
DESIGN: Karen Bartolomei

please
join
us
for
our
second
annual
wine
and
cheese
cocktail
party

saturday
december 14th
8:00 p.m.

69 crawford st.
watertown, ma
02472
(617) 926-6464

megan
and
carrie

0578 **DESIGN:** Megan Cooney

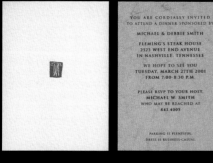

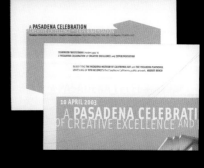

| 0579 | Anderson Thomas Design **DESIGN:** Jay Smith | 0581 | KBDA **DESIGN:** Keith Kneuven, Ramon Leander |
| 0580 | Gunter Advertising **DESIGN:** Sarah Grimm | 0582 | UTurn Design **DESIGN:** Stephanie Zelman |

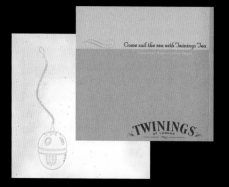

| 0583 | 9Spot Monk Design Co.
DESIGN: Vivian Leung | 0585 | 9Spot Monk Design Co.
DESIGN: Vivian Leung |
| 0584 | Graphic Type Services
DESIGN: Ravit Advocat | 0586 | Sayles Graphic Design
DESIGN: John Sayles, Som Inthalangsy |

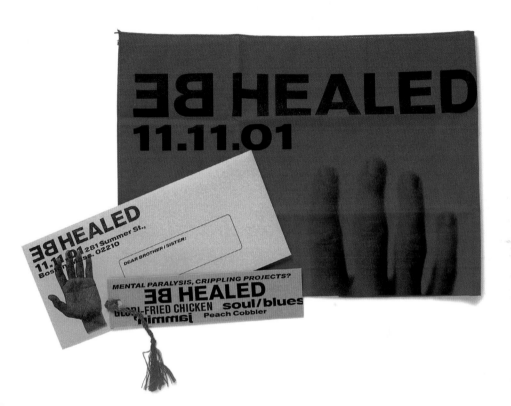

0587 | Rick Rawlins/Work
DESIGN: Rick Rawlins

0588 | **DESIGN:** Laura Ploszaj

Rule29
DESIGN: Justin Ahrens, Jon McGrath

0590   Sagmeister, Inc.
        DESIGN: Hjalti Karlsson

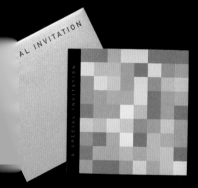 

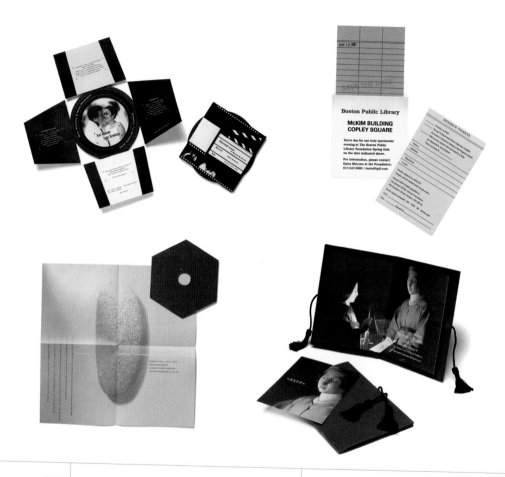

MARINATED FRESH
mozzarella
AND SWEET CHERRY TOMATOES
SERVED ON A BED OF BABY GREENS
TOSSED IN A BLOOD
O R A N G E
V I N A I G R E T T E A N D
ITALIAN B R E A D

ARTICHOKE
RAVIOLI
SMOKED

WITH
AND
R
RED

CHOCOLATE MOCHA & TIRAMISU

R.S.V.P.

THE FAVOUR OF A REPLY IS REQUESTED
BEFORE THE SEVENTEENTH OF AUGUST

*Name*_____

___ *Don't despair, will be there*

___ *Sad to say, will miss the day*

0599 **DESIGN:** Jennifer Hugunin

Juicy Temples Creative
DESIGN: Klaus Heesch, Mike Fusco

0601 energy energy design
DESIGN: Stacy Guidice,
Jeanette Aramburu

0602 Wages Design, Inc.
DESIGN: Joanna Tak

0603 Russell Design
DESIGN: Laura Ploszaj

0604 Pangaro Beer
DESIGN: David Salafia

| 0605 | Roycroft Design **DESIGN:** Jennifer Roycroft | 0607 | Egg Creatives **DESIGN:** Jason Che |
| 0606 | Top Design Studio **DESIGN:** Peleg Top, Rebekah Beaton | 0608 | Bah! Design **DESIGN:** Scott Herron, Lindsey Taylor |

Mirko Ilić Corp.
DESIGN: Mirko Ilić, Heath Hindgardner

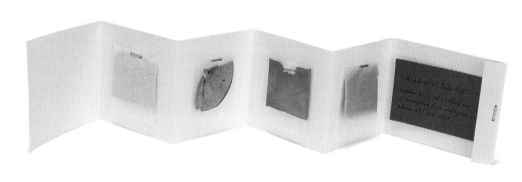

0610   **DESIGN:** Ann Conneman

 stavros
 is
 turning
 40

 come
 celebrate
 with
 cocktails & hors d'oevres

 and music
 by kid capri
 thursday march 4th @ 9
 at morton's

 rsvp
margaret maldonado
(310) 535-6145

0619 Design Dairy
DESIGN: H. Locascio

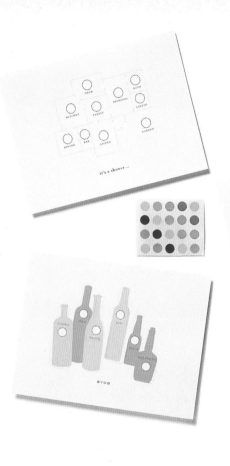

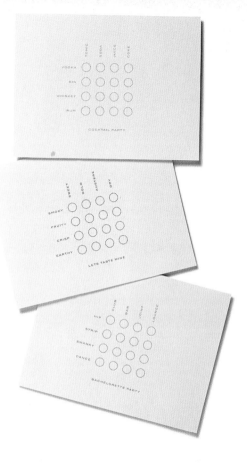

Greta Berger
DESIGN: Greta Berger

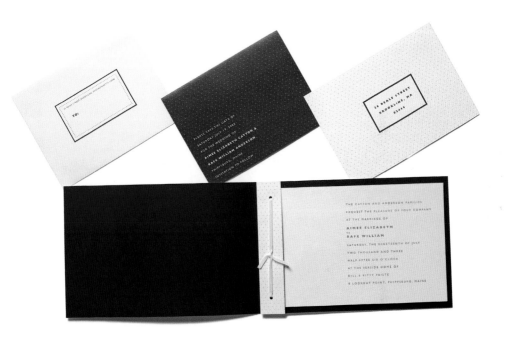

0633 | Brookline Street Design, Ltd.
DESIGN: Heather Snyder Quinn

0634   inpraxis, raum fur gestaltung
DESIGN: A. Kranz, C. Schaffner

0635	KO création **DESIGN:** Dennis Dulude	0637	Russell Design **DESIGN:** Laura Ploszaj
0636	Refinery Design Company **DESIGN:** Mike Schmalz	0638	Gutierrez Design Associates **DESIGN:** Jeannette Gutierrez

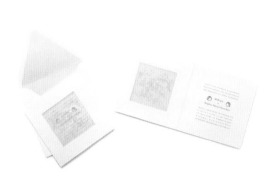

0639	Grapevine **DESIGN:** Karen Bartolomei	0641	Grapevine **DESIGN:** Karen Bartolomei
0640	Milk Row Studio/Press **DESIGN:** Keith D. Cross	0642	Wages Design, Inc. **DESIGN:** Matthew Taylor

Kehoe & Kehoe Design Associates
DESIGN: Lori Myers

0644   SiSu Design
DESIGN: Jennifer Stucker

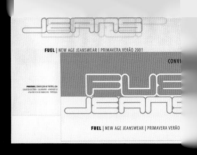

Bah! Design	0651	MA & Associados
DESIGN: Scott Herron, Rob Seale		**DESIGN:** Mario Aurelio
University of San Diego	0652	Pangaro Beer
DESIGN: Barbara Ferguson		**DESIGN:** David Salafia

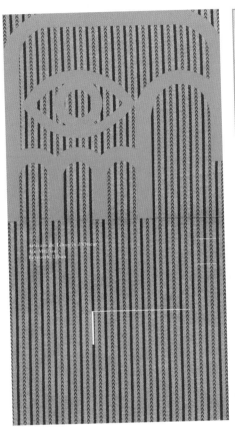

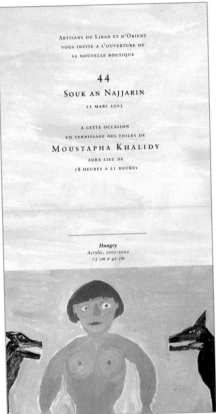

0653   Nassar Design
DESIGN: Margarita Encomienda, Nelida Nassar

0654

The Commissary
DESIGN: Lucas Charles

| 0655 | Sagmeister Inc.
DESIGN: Matthias Arnstberger | 0657 | Gutierrez Design Associates
DESIGN: Jeannette Gutierrez |
| 0656 | **DESIGN:** Julie Vail Maw | 0658 | AKA Design
DESIGN: Amy Ray |

0659   Visual Dialogue
DESIGN: Fritz Klaetke

0660   Wages Design, Inc.
DESIGN: Joanna Tak

0661   Donegan Creative
DESIGN: Lorraine Donegan

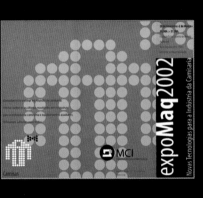

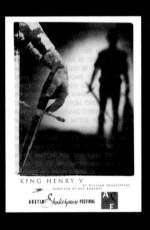

| 0662 | Stereobloc
DESIGN: Maik Brummundt | 0664 | Stereobloc
DESIGN: Maik Brummundt |
| 0663 | MA & Associados
DESIGN: Mario Aurelio | 0665 | Bah! Design
DESIGN: Scott Herron |

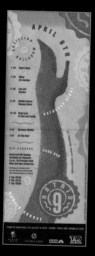

0670 Liquid Agency, Inc.
DESIGN: Julia Held

0671

Sayles Graphic Design
DESIGN: John Sayles, Som Inthalangsy

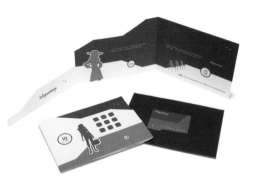

0672	Brookline Street Design, Ltd. **DESIGN:** Heather Snyder Quinn	0674	Grapevine **DESIGN:** Karen Bartolomei
0673	Kolegram Design **DESIGN:** Annie Tanguay, Gontran Blais	0675	Anderson Thomas Design **DESIGN:** Jay Smith

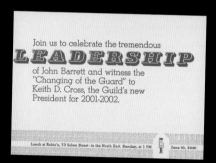

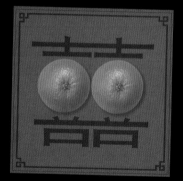

0676	Brookline Street Design, Ltd. **DESIGN:** Heather Snyder Quinn	0678	Brookline Street Design, Ltd. **DESIGN:** Heather Snyder Quinn
0677	Milk Row Studio/Press **DESIGN:** Keith D. Cross	0679	Egg Creatives **DESIGN:** Lim Choon Pin

0680

Tom Fowler, Inc.
DESIGN: Thomas G. Fowler, Karl S. Maruyama

0681   Love Communication
DESIGN: Craig Lee

0682   Rick Rawlins/Work
DESIGN: Rick Rawlins

0683   Brookline Street Design, Ltd.
DESIGN: Heather Snyder Quinn

0684   Pernsteiner Creative Group, Inc.
DESIGN: Andy Hauck

Foundry Sports Medicine + Fitness

Grand Opening
for

Wednesday   June 4th, 2003   8:00 pm

FOUNDRY
SPORTS MEDICINE & FITNESS

Start your engines for The Neo-Futurists' 30 Bands in 60 Minutes!

30 Bands

Thursday FEBruary 22 2001

60 Minutes

at the metro
3730 n clark, chicago

convite
[groove is in the heart!]

Nuno Cacho
Pedro Tabuada
Quinta-Feira, 13.03.2003

April 5, 2002   5:00 p.m.
Piner Auditorium

Landscape Architecture:
Women in Practice

Carol R. Johnson / Mary Margaret Jones / Victoria Marshall / Martha Schwartz / Laura Solano

please join us for a
BLUE HOLIDAY PARTY

Cocktails and Dinner
Friday, November 15, 2002

Blue Inc
180 8th Avenue, Brooklyn, NY

R.S.V.P. 718.822.8354

SIBLING

RIVALRY

Some Assembly Requir

collage
CULTURE

ISABEL MINNEMANN SANTOS E JAIME RAMALHO SANTOS
ELISA GALANTE GONÇALVES E JOSÉ GOMES GONÇALVES

Têm o prazer de vos convidar para o casamento de
seus filhos, MARTA E RICARDO GIL, que se realiza a 17
de Novembro, às 12:15 H, na Igreja de S. João Baptista
da Foz do Douro

R.S.F.F 93 101 23 91 / 96 239 61 22

0693 | R2 design
DESIGN: Lize Defossez Ramalho, Artur Rebelo

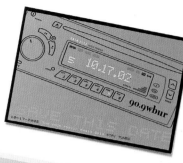

The WBUR Public Radio Gala

Hosted by NPR's SCOTT SIMON

wbur PUBLIC RADIO
g A L @

with special guests
DANIEL SCHORR
WALTER CRONKITE

October 17, 2002
Four Seasons Hotel, Boston

90.9wbur

2002:
[October 17, to be exact]

wbur PUBLIC RADIO
g A L @

Celebrate
public
broadcasting
at the
Four Seasons Hotel,
Boston

0694 | Cahoots
DESIGN: Michael Bouchard

Tupperware POKER PARTY

{ november 15 }

7 - 9 DINNER & SHOW
9 - ? CARDS

1211 EDGEWOOD
NORTHBROOK, IL 60062
RSVP 847-490-0702

please join us to celebrate when our daughter

Elizabeth Anne

celebrate

YES INDEED, **IT'S** GAST
RONOMIC **TICKLE** TIME
AGAAIN! KRIST**I**N AND
LANNY SOMMESE IN
VITE YOU TO SOME GR
EAT EATS AND A **GOO**D
FORK'IN **TIME** AT THE
EGGGSPENSE OF SOMM
ESE DEESIGN. NIN**E** P.M
AT MARIO AND **LUIGI'S**
ON NOVEMBER EIGHTH
CALL SOON! 814.353.195

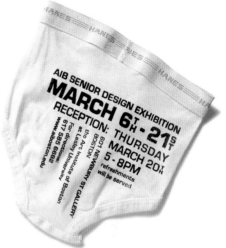

Oh Crap. THE REAL WORLD

AIB SENIOR DESIGN EXHIBITION
MARCH 6TH - 21ST
RECEPTION: THURSDAY MARCH 20TH
5 - 8PM
at Lesley University of Boston
the Art Institute of Boston
601 NEWBURY ST GALLERY
BOSTON
For directions:
617 585 6682
www.aiboston.edu
refreshments
will be served

0703 | **DESIGN:** Prank

TO ENCOURAGE YOU THROUGH ALL THE CHANGES OF YOUR LIVES TO ENCOURAGE

TO TOLERATE YOUR EVER-EXPANDING MUSIC COLLECTION TO TOLERATE YOUR

JOIN US

TO SHARE MY LIFE OPENLY WITH YOU TO SHARE MY LIFE OPENLY WITH YOU TO

TO BE PATIENT WITH YOU WHEN YOU'RE ACTING NUTS TO BE PATIENT WITH YOU

FRESH — *Enjoy* — TASTY

BRUNCH

WITH THE

NEWLYWEDS

OPEN HOUSE · 12 noon to 4 o'clock · FRIDAY, JULY 5

hosted by the mother of the bride

AT HER LAKEFRONT HOME IN NEWTON, NJ

DRIVING DIRECTIONS ON BACK · PLEASE RSVP OR ENCLOSED CARD

RED, WHITE AND I BOX
LETTERPRESS PRINTED BY THE BRIDE IN NEW YORK CITY
IN A NUMBERED EDITION OF 68
N° 2

The PLEASURE OF YOUR COMPANY IS REQUESTED AS

jennifer juliano
AND
richard orlando

EXCHANGE WEDDING VOWS AND
BECOME HUSBAND AND WIFE

THURSDAY
THE FOURTH OF JULY
2002
AT HALF AFTER THREE
IN THE
AFTERNOON

APPLE VALLEY INN · GLENWOOD NEW JERSEY
FEAST AND FESTIVITIES TO FOLLOW

music·mingle
toast·chat
eat·drink·
dance·relax
family·friends
·live·love·laugh·

0704 Jennifer Juliano Art, Design
DESIGN: Jennifer Juliano

| 0705 | Anvil Graphic Design, Inc.
DESIGN: Lori Rosales | 0707 | Yee-Ping Cho Design
DESIGN: Yee-Ping Cho |
| 0706 | Becker Design
DESIGN: Neil Becker | 0708 | Vrontikis Design Office
DESIGN: Kim Sage |

0709	Viñas Design **DESIGN:** Jaime Viñas	0711	Grapevine **DESIGN:** Karen Bartolomei
0710	Free Association **DESIGN:** Jason Fairchild	0712	Brookline Street Design, Ltd. **DESIGN:** Heather Snyder Quinn

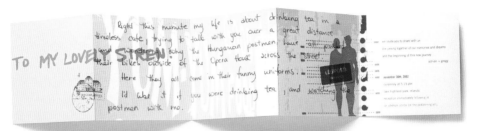

Right this minute my life is about drinking tea in a timeless cafe, trying to talk with you over a great distance and wondering why the Hungarian postmen have all parked their bikes outside of the Opera House across the street.

Here they all come in their funny uniforms.

I'd like it if you were drinking tea, and watching the postmen with me.

TO MY LOVELY SIREN:

-You gave me two blue bottles once.
I still have one of them. I like it.
You can see through it, and everything looks so peaceful. Almost like watching the world float underwater.

-I wonder if you chased little girls around the schoolyard?

-Sometimes I remember you late at night
When I do remember you,
I wonder if you are real
or if you are just a ghost
from my past.

-Would you hop a train?

-We stayed up half the night under a half lit moon giggling about Mercury, and Jupiter, and the looney-tunes characters.
Did you have half as much fun as I did?

Dec 1996

Hello?

You said once, maybe twice,
that you felt destined to know me.
Your socio-political anxiis being what they are,
I would be foolish to question your wisdom.
I'm not really sure I feel dangerous
but the tea is nice and it smells sweet.
Sweet like a teacher's poem.
Sweet like friendship.
Sweet like letting someone know you.

It's late (early) and the light is yellow
and the steam twists up like old, heavy memories.

We have a morning to know each other.

Hello.

May 1999

we invite you to share with us
the joining together of our memories and dreams
and the beginning of this new journey

adrien + gregg

november 30th, 2002
ceremony at 5:15 pm
near highland park, illinois
reception immediately following at
dr. prehn's castle (in the sustaining arts)

July 2002

0714   **DESIGN:** Julie Vail Maw

Together with their families

karen lynn sackman &
stephan michael farber

invite you to join in the celebration of their marriage

Saturday, the twentieth of September 2003
at half past six o'clock

WAVE HILL
RIVERDALE, NEW YORK

Dinner and dancing
to follow

IT'S TIME FOR A
ONE-OF-A-KIND
CELEBRATION.

JOIN US FOR OUR ALL-OUT-ART
25TH ANNIVERSARY PARTY

2001 SHATTUCK AWARDS SHATTUCK AWARDS SHATTUCK

HENRY L. SHATTUCK
PUBLIC SERVICE AWARDS
BOSTON MUNICIPAL RESEARCH BUREAU

LET'S SHOWER OUR BRIDE TO BE

Ghazal Melody

Sunday, August 17th, 2003
at two o'clock

HOSTED BY

Azita Emami
177 GLASGOW
SAN CARLOS, CALIFORNIA

Rsvp
BY AUGUST 1 • 650 – 802 – 8256

| 0715 | Ecrie **DESIGN:** Camilla Sorenson | 0717 | Bah! Design **DESIGN:** Scott Herron |
| 0716 | Mirage Design **DESIGN:** Lynette Allaire | 0718 | Ecrie **DESIGN:** Camilla Sorenson |

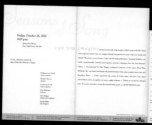

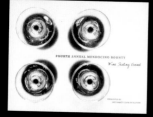

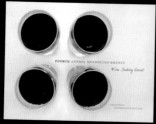

Additional Information

Heather and Joe
invite you
to their wedding ceremony
Saturday, June eighth
Two Thousand and
at four o'clock in the afternoon
Marconi Beach Station
Wellfleet, MA
Celebration to follow

HEATHER & JOE

Gail & Jay Dorsey
8 Roundy Rd
Lynnfield, MA 01940

0723 | Brookline Street Design, Ltd.
DESIGN: Heather Snyder Quinn

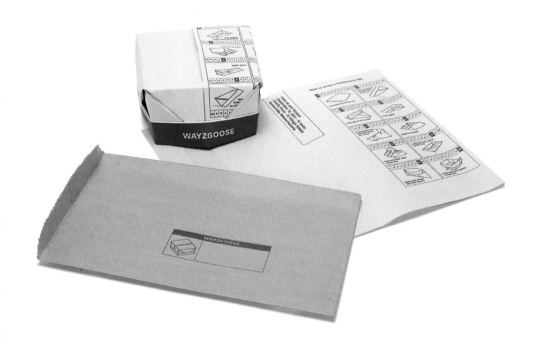

0724

Rick Rawlins/Work
DESIGN: Rick Rawlins, Manuel Ortega

We hope you will be able to join us
ON OUR WEDDING DAY
September 13, 2003
AT THE JACKSON HOUSE INN
Woodstock, Vermont

ASHLEY BAXTER & ERIC BARTLETT
invitation to follow

Hotel information

WOODSTOCK INN AND RESORT $250.00*
Fourteen The Green, Woodstock
802.457.1100 toll free 800.448.7900 www.woodstockinn.com

THE SHIRE MOTEL $90-150*
46 Pleasant Street, Woodstock
802.457.2211 www.shiremotel.com

FOR MORE INFORMATION
Visit www.woodstockvt.com or call toll free 888.496.6378 for availability

* To receive the special room rates listed above, please mention the Baxter/Bartlett Wedding
when making your reservations

ASHLEY
& ERIC

0726   Kolegram Design
DESIGN: Jean-Francois Plante

0727	Bah! Design **DESIGN:** Scott Herron	0729	Greteman Group **DESIGN:** Garrett Fresh
0728	Design 5 **DESIGN:** Tessa Schafer	0730	**DESIGN:** Anne-Lise Dermenghem

0731 Bandujo, Donker & Brothers
DESIGN: Laum Astuto

0732 Lloyds Graphic Design
DESIGN: Alexander Lloyd

0733 Alterpop
DESIGN: Todd Verlander, Kimberly Powell

0734 **DESIGN:** Sayre Gaydos

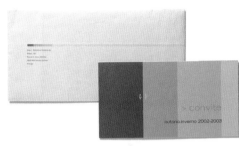

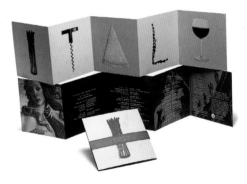

0735	Gutierrez Design Associates **DESIGN:** Jeannette Gutierrez	0737	MA & Associados **DESIGN:** Mario Aurelio
0736	AKA Design **DESIGN:** Stacy Lanier	0738	John Kneapler Design **DESIGN:** Niccole White

1 febbraio 2003 Tecla Magnoni e Italo Zuccari si sposano.

0739 INOX Design
DESIGN: Masa Magnoni

Wir heiraten am 22. Dezember 2001
im Standesamt Zürich. Die Feier findet
in familiärem Rahmen statt.

Zu unserem großen Hochzeitsfest
am 11. Mai 2002 im Schloss Au
am Zürichsee laden wir herzlich ein.

Wir bitten um eine schnelle Antwort
bis spätestens Ende Februar 2002.

Birthe Böttger ✂ *Martin Sohm*

0740   **DESIGN:** Maren Bottger

0741   Garfinkel Design
DESIGN: Wendy Garfinkel-Gold

PAUL LEIBOW

PARKER GALLERY
Thursday, April 3rd · 6-8 pm

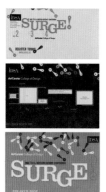

0746	AKA Design **DESIGN:** Lauren Anderson	0748	Leibow Studios **DESIGN:** Paul Leibow
0747	Sire Design	0749	Kevin Akers, Design & I...

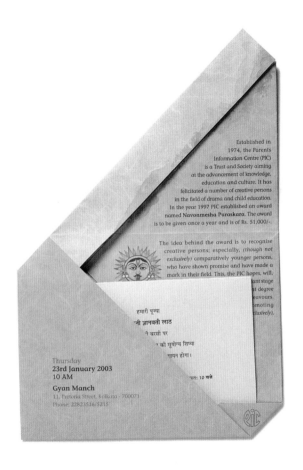

Established in
1974, the Parents
Information Centre (PIC)
is a Trust and Society aiming
at the advancement of knowledge,
education and culture. It has
felicitated a number of creative persons
in the field of drama and child education.
In the year 1997 PIC established an award
named **Navonmesha Puraskara**. The award
is to be given once a year and is of Rs. 51,000/-.

The idea behind the award is to recognise
creative persons; especially, *(though not
exclusively)* comparatively younger persons,
who have shown promise and have made a
mark in their field. This, the PIC hopes, will,
ant stage
nt degree
eavours.
omoting
clusively),

हमारी पूज्या

त्री ज्ञानवती लाठ

ने बरसी पर

र को सुयोग्य शिष्या

गायन होगा।

Thursday
23rd January 2003
10 AM

Gyan Manch
11, Pretoria Street, Kolkata - 700071
Phone: 22823516/5215

गत: **10 बजे**

0750   Appropriate Design
DESIGN: Shivani and Sanjeev Bothra

0751 Selbert Perkins Design
DESIGN: Sheri Bates

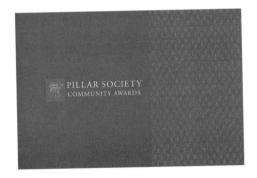

0752	Anvil Graphic Design, Inc. **DESIGN:** Gary Wong	0754	Pangaro Beer **DESIGN:** David Salafia, Joanna DeFazio
0753	Design 5 **DESIGN:** Chris DuBurg	0755	Bah! Design **DESIGN:** Scott Herron, Rob Seale

0756	Special Modern Design **DESIGN:** Karen Barranco	0758	Barbara Brown Marketing & Design **DESIGN:** Jon A. Leslie
0757	Concrete, Chicago **DESIGN:** Jilly Simons, Regan Todd	0759	Visual Dialogue **DESIGN:** Fritz Klaetke

0760	UP Creative Design & Advertising Co. **DESIGN:** Andy Lee	0762	Popcorn Initiative **DESIGN:** Chris Jones, Roger Wood
0761	Transcend **DESIGN:** Hung Q. Tran	0763	UP Creative Design & Advertising Co. **DESIGN:** Ben Wang

Partners in Print
DESIGN: Ariel Janzen

0765 Palo Alto Junior Museum & Zoo
DESIGN: Efrat Rafaeli

0766 Firebelly Design Co.
DESIGN: Dawn Hancock

0767 Aadvert International
DESIGN: Heather Schulein

0768 Design 5
DESIGN: Chris DuBurg

SANTA BARBARA
MUSEUM OF
ART

1130 STATE STREET
SANTA BARBARA, CA 93101-2746
www.sbmuseart.org

YOU'RE INVITED

TO SEE...

David Alfaro Siqueiros,
born and died Mexico,
1898–1974 (active Mexico,
United States, France, and
Spain), Retrato del México
de hoy (Portrait of Mexico
Today), 1932. Casein oil
pigment on cement applied
to plaster, 32' x 8' x 6'.
Anonymous gift. Funding
for transportation and con-
servation of this Siqueiros
mural was provided by two
anonymous donors.

0773 Barbara Brown Marketing & Design
DESIGN: Jon A. Leslie

0774 | Riordon Design
DESIGN: Cori Hellard, Tim Warnock

Juicy Temples Creative
DESIGN: Klaus Heesch, Mike Fusco

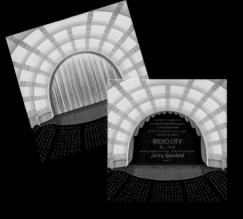

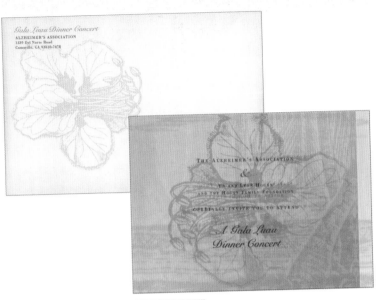

Gala Luau Dinner Concert
ALZHEIMER'S ASSOCIATION
1339 Del Norte Road
Camarillo, CA 93010-7478

THE ALZHEIMER'S ASSOCIATION
&
ED AND LYNN HOGAN
AND THE HOGAN FAMILY FOUNDATION

CORDIALLY INVITE YOU TO ATTEND

A Gala Luau Dinner Concert

A Gala Luau Dinner Concert

HONORING
Martha K. Smith
(MRS. MARTIN V. SMITH)

FEATURING THE KINGSTON TRIO
WITH WE FIVE AND CELEBRITY HOST BOB EUBANKS

NAME
ADDRESS
CITY   STATE   ZIP
TELEPHONE

☐ I would like to reserve _____ tickets at $150 per person.

☐ I am unable to attend but would like to make a donation of $_____ to The Alzheimer's Association.

☐ CHECK ENCLOSED   ☐ VISA   ☐ MASTERCARD

CREDIT CARD NUMBER   EXP.
NAME AS IT APPEARS ON CREDIT CARD
SIGNATURE REQUIRED

For IRS purposes Value received per person is $100. The balance of your contribution is a gift to The Alzheimer's Association. Please make checks payable to *The Alzheimer's Association*. For more information, please call The Alzheimer's Association, Ventura County Chapter, (805) 485-5597.

PLEASE RSVP BY JUNE 5, 2002

0780 | Barbara Brown Marketing & Design
DESIGN: Alicia Hoskins

0781   Insight Design Communications
DESIGN: Lea Carmichael

0790   **DESIGN:** Ann Conneman

0791

Art Center College of Design
DESIGN: Triana The

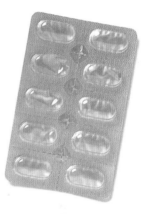

AIDS IN SOUTH AFRICA
The Social Expression of a Pandemic
19-20 april 2002, Wellesley College USA

You are cordially invited to a conference on the social,
economic, and human impact of AIDS in South Africa.
International experts will attend and present their work.
Registration is required for limited spaces. Please confirm
your attendance by calling 781 283 2159.

Lectures and Cultural Events Offices; Dean Fund for World Citizen; Knapp Social
Science Center; Presidential Discretionary Fund; Mildred Lane Kemper Art Museum; Latin
American and International Departments; AK Bayerman Institute; Women's Studies; Sociology
Anthropology and Education; Medical Anthropology; Multicultural Education & Diversity Initiatives

FRI / 19 APR

16h00   Keynote Address / Jewett Auditorium
         Jeffrey Sachs -Harvard University
         Sonia Ehrich Sachs - Pediatrician

20h30   South African AIDS Film / Collins Cinema
         Shouting Silent with producer Xoliswa Sithole

SAT / 20 APR

         Main Conference Sessions / Pendleton Hall
         Howard Phillips - University of Cape Town
8h30   Putting HIV/AIDS in Historical Perspective

         Video Link / Living with HIV/AIDS

7h30   a) Cal Volks - University of Cape Town
         HIV/AIDS and South African Universities

7h30   b) Jeffrey Lewis -World Bank
         The Economic Impact of AIDS on South Africa

         Marilyn Martin - South African National Gallery
         AIDS and the South African Art Community

         a) Claudia Cruz - University of Cape Town
         The Anthropology of Condom Use in South Africa

         b) Virginia van d'Vliet - AIDS Alert
         Politics and the AIDS Crisis in South Africa

0800   Rick Rawlins/Work
        DESIGN: Rick Rawlins

0801   Pure Imagination Studios
        DESIGN: Josh Williams

0802　Chen Design Associates
DESIGN: Max Spector

0803   Watts Design
DESIGN: Peter Watts

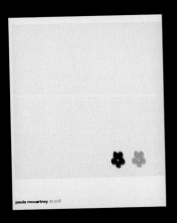

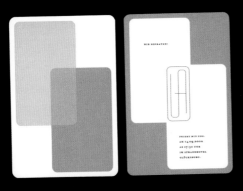

Please Save the Date

August 23, 2003

For the Wedding of

Jennifer Ann Grochowalski &

Christian Mark Dadagian

in Newport, Rhode Island

PLEASE JOIN US

FOR A BRUNCH

SATURDAY, JUNE 14TH

AT THE HOME OF

ANN AND JOHN JAMES

FROM 11-2

PLEASE RSVP

Directions, from the center of Carlisle, MA
Take school street up the hill, past the church
Take a left onto Baldwin Rd.
56 Baldwin Rd is the first house on the right.

0808	Russell Design **DESIGN:** Dana Snider	0810	Sayles Graphic Design **DESIGN:** John Sayles, Som Inthalangsy
0809	Brookline Street Design, Ltd. **DESIGN:** Heather Snyder Quinn	0811	Brookline Street Design, Ltd. **DESIGN:** Heather Snyder Quinn

MR. AND MRS. ROBERT P. HUNT
105 H STREET
SOUTH BOSTON, MASSACHUSETTS
0 2 1 2 7

Rsvp

MR/MRS/MS.

ACCEPTS
REGRETS

BEFORE SEPTEMBER TWENTIETH

AT TWENTY MINUTES TO ELEVEN O'CLOCK
SATURDAY, THE THIRD OF AUGUST, TWO THOUSAND AND TWO

Karen Marie Bartolomei
AND
Robert Francis Hunt

EXCHANGED MARRIAGE VOWS AND WERE UNITED AS HUSBAND AND WIFE
IN MICHELANGELO'S PIAZZA DEL CAMPIDOGLIO
ROME, ITALY

THEY WILL RETURN FROM THEIR HONEYMOON IN PARIS, FRANCE
SATURDAY, THE TENTH OF AUGUST

0812 Grapevine
DESIGN: Karen Bartolomei

Brookline Street Design, Ltd.
DESIGN: Heather Snyder Quinn

0814

Blue Inc.
DESIGN: Tracey Chiang

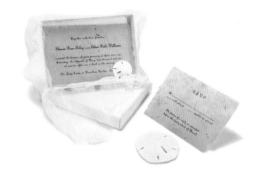

a bridal shower for dana

new years day
at four o'clock
15 claremont avenue, apartment 32
new york city   10027

rsvp to carolyn by december 22
415.346.8647 or Carolyn_Hack@hotmail.com

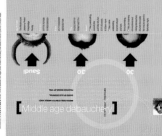

[Middle age debauchery]

convite | invitation

THE FAVOUR OF A REPLY IS REQUESTED
BEFORE THE NINTH OF JUNE

M

WILL _____ ATTEND

NUMBER OF PERSONS ATTENDING _____

0819	Smudge Ink **DESIGN:** Kate Saliba	0821	Wilson Harvey **DESIGN:** Paul Burgess
0820	MA & Associados **DESIGN:** Mari...Aurelia	0822	The Commissary **DESIGN:** Lucas Cha...a...

PLEASE JOIN US WHEN OUR SON

ANDREW SPENCER

IS CALLED TO THE TORAH

SATURDAY, THE THIRTY-FIRST OF MAY
TWO THOUSAND AND THREE
AT TEN-THIRTY IN THE MORNING
CHELSEA PIERS - PIER SIXTY
NEW YORK, NEW YORK

LUNCHEON WILL FOLLOW SERVICE

LEIGH & CHARLES MERINOFF

| 0823 | Brookline Street Design, Ltd.
DESIGN: Heather Snyder Quinn | 0825 | Refinery Design Company
DESIGN: Julie Schmalz |
| 0824 | **DESIGN:** Sayre Gaydos | | |

0826   Muzak Marketing
DESIGN: David Eller

With joyous hearts, your presence is hereby requested to join Scott & Tracy in a celebration of love to be held at Daniels Summit Pass, Highway 40, Heber City, Utah, located in the United States of America. Visit www.danielssummit.com for information.

0831

angryporcupine_design
DESIGN: Cheryl Roder-Quill

0832 Ideas Frescas
DESIGN: Lee Newham

ANNIE TAYLOR & ANTON INGHAM
ARE GETTING HITCHED!

SAVE THE DATE

WE ARE GETTING MARRIED
AUGUST 31ST 2002, NYC.

PLEASE JOIN US!

**lindsey and hudd
have two lawn chairs**

for their graduation party, so you better bring your own because you are invited to help them celebrate on may forth two thousand and three from three o'clock until you get tired of sitting at shelby forest state park shelter number three.

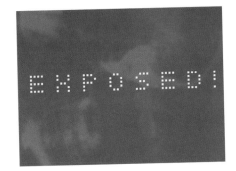

0833   Peter Kruty Editions
DESIGN: Sayre Gaydos

0834   The Commissary
DESIGN: Hudd Byard

0835   Anvil Graphic Design, Inc.
DESIGN: Lori Rosales

0836   Barbara Brown Marketing & Design
DESIGN: Carole Brooks

Massachusetts High Technology Council

ANNUAL MEETING
& DINNER IN HONOR OF HOWARD P. FOLEY

0837	Mirage Design **DESIGN:** Lynette Allaire	0839	Yee-Ping Cho Design **DESIGN:** Yee-Ping Cho
0838	**DESIGN:** Rob Kimmell	0840	re:salzman Designs **DESIGN:** Rick Salzman, Ida Cheinman

0841	Ecrie **DESIGN:** Camilla Sorenson	0843	Barbara Brown Marketing & Design **DESIGN:** Alicia Hoskins
0842	Alterpop **DESIGN:** Kimberly Powell	0844	Wages Design, Inc. **DESIGN:** Diane Kim

0845 Simply Put Design
DESIGN: Carrene Tracy

0846	M-Art **DESIGN:** Marty Ittner	0848	graphische formgebung **DESIGN:** Herbert Rohsiepe
0847	UP Creative Design & Advertising Co. **DESIGN:** Ben Wang	0849	Rick Johnson & Company **DESIGN:** Tim McGrath

0854

Insight Design Communications
DESIGN: Lea Carmichael

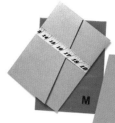

0855	IE Design	0857	IE Design
	DESIGN: Amy Klass, Cya Nelson		**DESIGN:** Cya Nelson
0856	EM Press	0858	Riordon Design
	DESIGN: Elias Roustom		**DESIGN:** Sharon Pece

| 0859 | Becker Design
DESIGN: Kaytee Mosher | 0861 | Group 55 Marketing
DESIGN: Jeannette Gutierrez |
| 0860 | Sayles Graphic Design
DESIGN: John Sayles, Som Inthalangsy | 0862 | Rick Johnson & Company
DESIGN: Tim McGrath |

| 0863 | Greteman Group **DESIGN:** Craig Tomson | 0865 | Bandujo, Donker & Brothers **DESIGN:** Connie Dennis |
| 0864 | R2 design **DESIGN:** Liza Defossez Ramalho, Artur Rebelo | 0866 | Concrete, Chicago **DESIGN:** Jilly Simons, Regan Todd |

0867   Bruketa & Zinic
DESIGN: Davor Bruketa, Nikola Zinic

0868

Blue Inc.
DESIGN: Tracey Chiang, Nina Max Daly

0869   **DESIGN:** Garet McIntyre

0870   Burgeff Co.
        DESIGN: Patride Burgeff

0871   Mike Quon/Designation
        DESIGN: Mike Quon

0872   Rick Rawlins/Work
        DESIGN: Rick Rawlins

The families of Juliette and Jeff invite you to a beach front barbeque
on the eve of forever after
Friday, September thirteenth, from 5 to 8 pm

CASUAL ATTIRE

The Celebration begins at a quarter to six o'clock
The Exchange of Vows will take place at seven o'clock, as the sun sets
Dinner and Dancing will follow

JACKETS PREFERRED

0873   Grapevine
        DESIGN: Karen Bartolomei

0874 | Greteman Group
DESIGN: Craig Tomson

SELF-PROMOTION

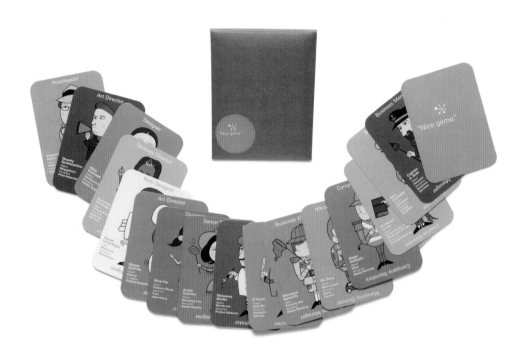

0875   That's Nice, LLC
DESIGN: David Phan, Scott Robertson, Elan Harris

0876

0877

0879

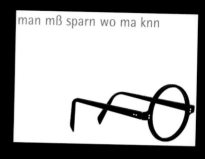

man mß sparn wo ma knn

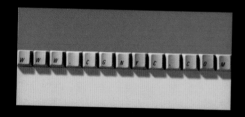

0880   Nassar Design
        DESIGN: M. Encomienda, N. Nassar

0881   Chermayeff & Geismar, Inc.
        DESIGN: Ian Perkins

0882   Baumann & Baumann
        DESIGN: Barbara & Geid Baumann

0883   Firebelly Design Co.
        DESIGN: Dawn Hancock

0884   KBDA
DESIGN: Liz Burrill

0885 | Muzak Marketing
DESIGN: David Eller

Dare to take time to smell the pine

0886	That's Nice, LLC **DESIGN:** Kaoru Kaojima	0888	Animated Graphix & Design **DESIGN:** Jamie Horner
0887	Gulla Design **DESIGN:** Steve Gulla	0889	Stahl Partners, Inc. **DESIGN:** David Stahl

0890

0892

0891

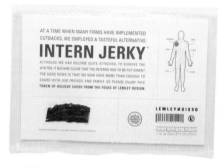

0893

| 0890 | Chen Design Associates
DESIGN: Max Spector, Joshua C. Chen,
Kathryn Hoffman | 0892 | Muzak Marketing
DESIGN: David Eller |
| 0891 | Russell Design
DESIGN: Julie Beard | 0893 | Lemley Design Company
DESIGN: David Lemley, Yuri Shuets |

0894 Greteman Group
DESIGN: James Strange, Craig Tomson

0895

0897

0896

0898

0899 Sayles Graphic Design
DESIGN: John Sayles, Som Inthalangsy

0900 Sky Design
DESIGN: Carrie Wallace

0901 Sayles Graphic Design
DESIGN: John Sayles, Som Inthalangsy

0902 Group 55 Marketing
DESIGN: Jeannette Gutierrez

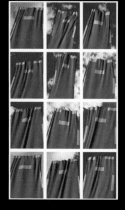

| 0903 | Studio International
DESIGN: Boris Liubicic | 0905 | Eastern Edge Media Group
DESIGN: M. J. Pressley-Jones |
| 0904 | KBDA
DESIGN: Jamie Diersing | 0906 | Momentum Press and Design
DESIGN: Jill Vartenigian |

wow.

know now.

know how.

0907 | Be Design
DESIGN: Eric Read

0908   Mirko Ilić Corp.
DESIGN: Mirko Ilić

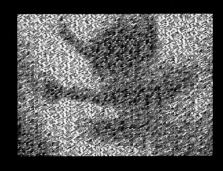

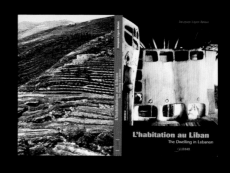

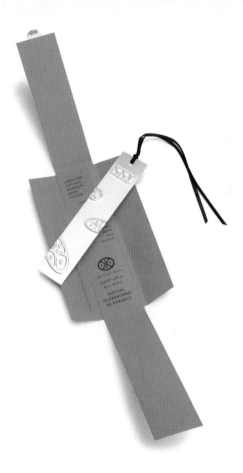

0917   Nassar Design
DESIGN: Margarita Encomienda, Nelida Nassar

0918 | Baumann & Baumann
DESIGN: Barbara and Geid Baumann

0919

0921

0920

0922

0919	Kolegram Design **DESIGN:** Mike Teixeira	0921	Baumann & Baumann **DESIGN:** Barbara and Geid Baumann
0920	Red Alert Design **DESIGN:** Jon Wainwright, Matt Sanderman	0922	Rick Rawlins/Work **DESIGN:** Rick Rawlins

0927 | IE Design
DESIGN: Amy Klass

0928

Michael Courtney Design
DESIGN: Michael Courtney, Karen Cramer, Heidi Favour, Margaret Long, Jennifer Comer, Lauren DiRusso

0933   Egg Creatives
DESIGN: Jason Chen

0934 Michael Osborne Design
DESIGN: Michelle Regenbogen

0935

0937

0936

0938

0939

Zappata Disenadores S.C.
DESIGN: Ibo Angulo

0940   Letter Design
DESIGN: Paul Shaw

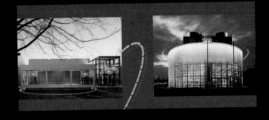

0941	BLANK, Inc. **DESIGN:** Robert Kent Wilson, Danielle Willis, Christine Oziecholowski	0943	Kevin Akers Design & Imagery **DESIGN:** Kevin Akers
0942	Firebelly Design Co. **DESIGN:** Mikel Rosenthal	0944	Nassar Design **DESIGN:** Margarita Encomienda, Nelida Nassar

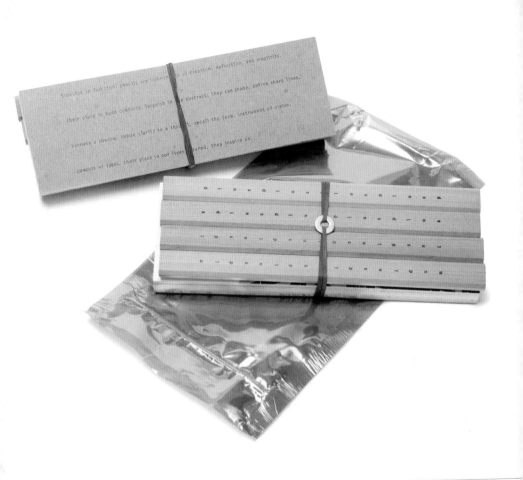

Idealistic in function, pencils are instruments of creation, definition, and simplicity.

their place in hand comforts. languish in our abstract; they can shade, define sharp lines.

barness a shadow. imbue clarity to a thought. recall the form. instrument of vision.

conduit of ideas, their place in our lives figured, they inspire us.

0949 plus design, inc.
DESIGN: Anita Meyer, Vivian Law, Karin Fickett, Kristin Hughes

0950 **DESIGN:** Vrontikis Design Office

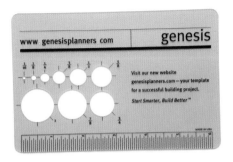

0951	Rick Rawlins/Work **DESIGN:** Rick Rawlins	0953	Hecht Design **DESIGN:** Elisa Rogers, Megan Verdugo
0952	Kevin Akers Design & Imagery **DESIGN:** Kevin Akers	0954	Louey/Rubino Design Group **DESIGN:** Robert Louey, Javier Leguizamo

0955   Rule 29
DESIGN: Justin Ahrens, Jim Boborci

EXPLORE
CREATE
INSPIRE

0956 Russell Design
DESIGN: Julie Beard

Robilant & Associates
DESIGN: Maurizio DiRobilant

Sayles Graphic Design
DESIGN: John Sayles, Som Inthalangsy

0959

Gutierrez Design Associates
DESIGN: Jeannette Gutierrez

0960

Greteman Group
DESIGN: James Strange, Craig Tomson

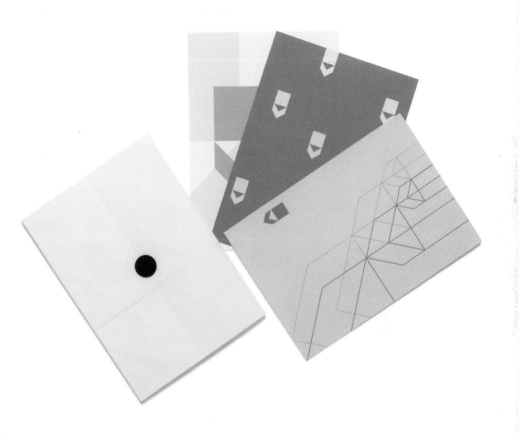

0961   Baumann & Baumann
DESIGN: Barbara and Geid Baumann

0962

Blue Inc.
DESIGN: Tracey Chiang

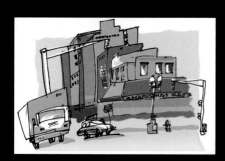

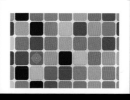

| 0963 | iNK design
 DESIGN: Wing Ngan, Maggie Cheung | 0965 | KO création
 DESIGN: Annie Lachapelle |
| 0964 | Stephen Burdick Design
 DESIGN: Stephen Burdick | 0966 | DC Design
 DESIGN: David Cater |

0971 **DESIGN:** Kinetik (Beth Clawson, Jeff Fabian, Beverley Hunter, Mike Joosse, Katie Kroener, Jackie Ratsch, Scott Rier, Sam Shelton, Jenny Skillman)

0972   OrangeSeed Design
DESIGN: Damien Wolf, Phil Hoch

...mery Vincent Design **DESIGN:** Emery Vincent	**0975** Stereobloc **DESIGN:** Udo Albrecht
...emley Design Company **DESIGN:** David Lemley, Yuri Shuets	**0976** Firebelly Design Co. **DESIGN:** Dawn Hancock

0977

Anvil Graphic Design, Inc.
DESIGN: Cathy Chin

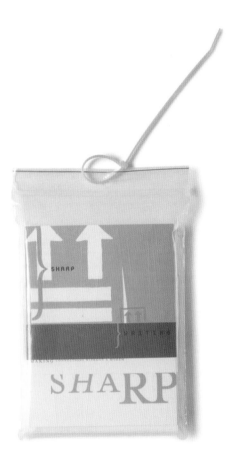

0978 **DESIGN:** Kinetik (Beth Clawson, Jeff Fabian, Beverley Hunter, Mike Joosse, Katie Kroener, Jackie Ratsch, Scott Rier, Sam Shelton, Jenny Skillman)

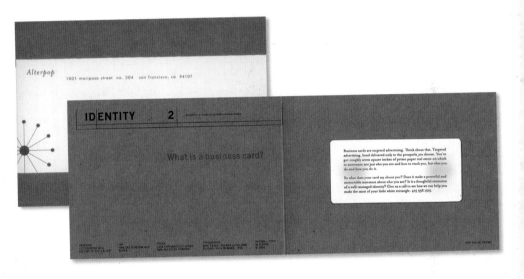

0984

Blue Inc.
DESIGN: Tracey Chiang

| 0985 | Grapevine
DESIGN: Karen Bartolomei | 0987 | ZGraphics, Ltd.
DESIGN: Renee Clark |
| 0986 | Acuity, Inc.
DESIGN: Lori Jenkins, Deena Holland | 0988 | Sommese Design
DESIGN: Lanny Sommese |

0989 Wallace Church, Inc.
DESIGN: John Bruno

NOW
MAKING
HOUSE
CALLS

STUDIO J
GRAPHIC
DESIGN
SERVICES

Specializing in marketing
and corporate identity

18 years experience

References available

To request a house call contact:

Angela Jackson, Studio J
(916) 348-8400
studioj@hotmail.com

0990   Studio J
DESIGN: Angela Jackson

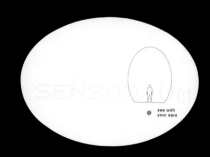

see with
your ears

0991	Kendall Ross **DESIGN:** David Kendall	0993	Sommese Design **DESIGN:** Lanny Sommese
0992	Burgeff Co. **DESIGN:** Patrick Burgeff	0994	Muzak Marketing **DESIGN:** David Eller

0995 Image Zoo
DESIGN: Jamie Flint

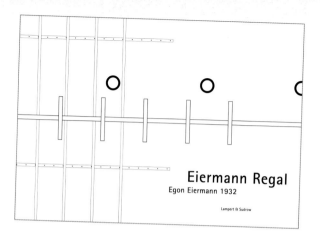

Eiermann Regal
Egon Eiermann 1932

Lampert & Sudrow

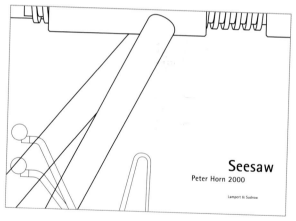

Seesaw
Peter Horn 2000

Lampert & Sudrow

0996   Baumann & Baumann
DESIGN: Barbara and Geid Baumann

Subject: emptiness
Purpose: our biggest challenge
Mission: fill out according to wishes

| 0997 | Nassar Design **DESIGN:** Margarita Encomienda, Nelida Nassar | 0999 | Rule 29 **DESIGN:** Justin Ahrens, Jim Boborci |
| | | 1000 | Graphic Type Services **DESIGN:** Ravit Advocat |

DIRECTORY

For contact information for the following design firms, please log on to Rockport Publishers' website, www.rockpub.com.

a

Aadvert International

0767
Art Director: Heather Schulein
Designer: Heather Schulein
Client: Sennheiser USA
Software/Hardware: Mac, Quark XPress,
Adobe Photoshop

Actia

0697
Art Director: Anne-Lise Dermenghem
Designer: Anne-Lise Dermenghem
Client: Actia
Software/Hardware: Quark XPress,
Adobe Photoshop,
Adobe Illustrator
Paper/Materials: Canevas/Thibierge
& Comar

Acuity, Inc.

0986
Art Director: Gail Tassell
Designers: Lori Jenkins, Deena Holland
Client: Acuity, Inc.
Software/Hardware: Adobe Illustrator,
Macromedia Flash, Mac
Paper/Materials: Silver Foil on Red
Paper, Interactive CD

ADVERSIS

0798
Art Director: Timo Wenda
Designers: Timo Wenda, Malthias Veith
Client: Malthias Veith
Software/Hardware: Quark Xpress

After Hours Creative

0142
Art Director: After Hours Creative
Designer: After Hours Creative
Client: Max & Lucy
Software/Hardware: Mac, Adobe
Illustrator

0350
Art Director: After Hours Creative
Designer: After Hourse Creative
Client: Osborn Maledon
Software/Hardware: Mac, Adobe
Illustrator, Adobe Photoshop

0721
Art Director: After Hours Creative
Designer: After Hours Creative
Client: Body Positive
Software/Hardware: Mac, Adobe
Photoshop

AKA Design

0736
Art Director: Stacy Lanier
Designer: Stacy Lanier
Client: McKendree College

0658
Art Director: Craig Simon
Designer: Amy Ray
Client: The Salvation Army

0746
Art Director: Craig Simon
Designer: Lauren Anderson
Client: Boys Hope Girls Hope

Alterpop

0414
Art Director: Doug Akagi
Designer: Christopher Simmons
Client: Elaine Shultz
Software/Hardware: Adobe Illustrator,
Mac
Paper/Materials: 4 Pt. Krome Cote

0449
Art Director: Doug Akagi
Designer: Christopher Simmons
Client: Alterpop
Software/Hardware: Adobe Illustrator,
Mac
Paper/Materials: 130 lb. Coronado
Double Thick

0842
Art Director: Dorothy Remington
Designer: Kimberly Powell
Client: California Academy of Sciences
Software/Hardware: Quark XPress, Mac
Paper/Materials: Recycled Paper,
Barbed Elastic Band,
Clear Plastic Envelope (Environmentally
Friendly), 80#
Coronado Cover (Paper)

0733
Art Director: Dorothy Remington
Designers: Todd Verlander, Kimberly
Powell
Client: California Academy of Sciences

Software/Hardware: Mac, Adobe
Illustrator
Paper/Materials: Sierra Paper

0983
Art Director: Doug Akagi
Designer: Christopher Simmons
Client: Alterpop
Software/Hardware: Adobe Illustrator,
Mac
Paper/Materials: Chip Board-1 color
offset, 1
rubber stamp, card-130 lb Coronado, 2
Color Letterpress, Low Tac Glue

And Partners

0243
Art Director: David Schimmel
Designer: David Schimmel
Client: AOL
Software/Hardware: Quark XPress,
Adobe Illustrator
Paper/Materials: Various

0328
Art Director: David Schimmel
Designer: David Schimmell
Client: David Schimmel & Partners
Software/Hardware: Quark XPress,
Adobe Illustrator
Paper/Materials: Neenah Classic Crest

0450
Art Director: David Schimmel
Designer: David Schimmel & Sarah
Hollowood
Client: HN Media & Marketing
Software/Hardware: Quark XPress,
Adobe Illustrator
Paper/Materials: Mohawk Superfine

Anderson Thomas Design

0428
Art Director: Joel Anderson
Designer: Kristi Smith
Client: Anderson Thomas Design
Software/Hardware: Mac G4, Quark
XPress
Paper/Materials: Tango 10 pt C25

0502
Art Director: Roy Roper
Designer: Roy Roper
Client: Clinic for Women
Software/Hardware: Mac G4, Quark
XPress, Adobe Photoshop
Paper/Materials: Mohawk Textures

0579
Art Director: Jay Smith
Designer: Jay Smith
Client: Rocketown Youth Services
Software/Hardware: Mac 64, Quark
XPress, Adobe Illustrator
Paper/Materials: Zanders Medley-
Hammer, T-2000 and Elephant Hide,
Custom Metallic Ink

0675
Art Director: Jay Smith
Designer: Jay Smith
Client: Rocketown Youth Services
Software/Hardware: Mac 64, Quark
XPress, Adobe Photoshop
Paper/Materials: Gilbert Esse

angryporcupine_design

0412
Art Director: Cheryl Roder-Quill
Designer: Cheryl Roder-Quill
Client: Lew & Kelly Wagman
Software/Hardware: Adobe Illustrator,
Mac
Paper/Materials: Neenah Classic Crest,
Chartham Translucents, Metal Rim Tags

0831
Art Director: Cheryl Roder-Quill
Designer: Cheryl Roder-Quill
Client: Scott lemon & Tracy Reinders
Software/Hardware: Adobe Illustrator,
Mac
Paper/Materials: Chartham Translucents,
Fox River, Confetti, Raffia

Animated Graphix & Design

0888
Art Director: Jamie Horner
Designer: Jamie Horner
Client: Mrs. Clark's Foods
Software/Hardware: Adobe Photoshop

Ann Conneman

0042, 0043
Designer: Ann Conneman
Paper/Materials: Stencilled paste paper
designs on Hahnemuhle Copperplate

0119
Designer: Ann Conneman
Paper/Materials: Hand-illustrated with
Prismacolor pencils

0129
Designer: Ann Conneman
Paper/Materials: Cromatica, chipboard, grommets

0470
Designer: Ann Conneman
Client: Gary Miller
Software/Hardware: Printed letterpress
Paper/Materials: Silver forks, cotton thread

0790
Designer: Ann Conneman
Client: Ann Conneman/John Cameron
Software/Hardware:Printed letterpress
Paper/Materials: Kitakata japanese paper, birch leaves, waxed linen thread, chipboard boxes

0610
Designer: Ann Conneman
Client: Gary Miller
Paper/Materials: Flour, apples, cinnamon, sugar, plastic bags, staples, Velke Losiny paper

Anvil Graphic Design, Inc.

0242
Art Directors: Laura Bauer, Roy Tabuma
Designers: Gary Wong, Cathy Chin
Client: Anvil
Software/Hardware: Adobe Illustrator 9.0,
Mac G4
Paper/Materials: Card-Mohawk Ultra Write Smooth 120# Envelope-Curious Metallics anodized

0719
Art Directors: Laura Bauer, Roy Tabuma
Designer: Cathy Chin
Client: Waldorf School
Software/Hardware: Adobe Illustrator 9.0, Mac 64
Paper/Materials: Mohawk Superfine Ultrasmooth 200# Cover

0752
Art Directors: Laura Bauer, Roy Tabuma
Designer: Gary Wong
Client: SFMOMA
Software/Hardware: Adobe Illustrator 9.0,
Mac G4
Paper/Materials: 100# Potlatch Scout Gloss Cover, 29# Curious Translucent

0705
Art Directors: Laura Bauer, Roy Tabuma
Designer: Lori Rosales
Client: Junior League
Software/Hardware: Adobe Illustrator 9.0,
Mac G4
Paper/Materials: Curious Metallics, Ice Gold
Test 80#

0835
Art Directors: Laura Bauer, Roy Tabuma
Designer: Lori Rosales
Client: Peter Herz
Software/Hardware: Adobe Illustrator 9.0,
Mac G4
Paper/Materials: Curious Metallics, Anodised Text 80lb.

0977
Art Directors: Laura Bauer, Roy Tabuma
Designer: Cathy Chin
Client: Aiga SF
Software/Hardware: Adobe Illustrator 9.0, Mac
Paper/Materials: Mohawk Superfine 130# Cover, Ultrawhite Eggshell

Appropriate Design

0750
Art Director: Sanjeev Bothra
Designers: Shivani and Sanjeev Bothra
Client: Neerja & Mukund Lath
Software/Hardware: Adobe Photoshop, Macromedia Freehand, PageMaker, Mac
Paper/Materials: Lucky Parchment Paper-Yellow 100 gsm, Lofty Natural Card 370 gsm

0897
Art Director: Sanjeev Bothra
Designer: Sanjeev Bothra
Client: Appropriate Design
Software/Hardware: Manual Illustration, Adopt Photoshop, PageMaker, Mac
Paper/Materials: TARA Hand Made Paper-Off White & Double Ply Black, String, Beads

Art Center College of Design

0791
Art Director: Gloria Kondrup
Designer: Triana The

Client: Ori, Origami Gallery
Software/Hardware: Macromedia Freehand, Mac
Paper/Materials: Stonehenge, Otis, Vellum, Onion Paper

ARTiculation Group

0005
Art Director: Joseph Chan
Designers: Joseph Chan, James Ayotte
Client: ARTiculation Group
Software/Hardware: Adobe Illustrator, Adobe Photoshop, Quark Xpress

0065, 0369
Art Director: Joseph Chan
Designers: Joseph Chan, James Ayotte
Client: WineCountry Vintners
Software/Hardware: Adobe Illustrator, Adobe Photoshop, Quark Xpress

0183
Art Director: Joseph Chan
Designers: Joseph Chan, Wilson Lam, Helen Ng, Karin Fukuzawa
Client: ARTiculation Group
Software/Hardware: Adobe Illustrator, Adobe Photoshop, Quark XPress
Paper/Materials: Bravo

Artistic Announcements

0240
Art Director: K.E. Roehr
Designer: K. E. Roehr
Client: The Rockwell Group
Software/Hardware: Adobe Illustrator, Mac
Paper/Materials: Strathmore, Puritan Press, Tru-Line Die Cutting

0565
Art Director: K. E. Roehr
Designer: K. E. Roehr
Client: Theresa & Ryan Luther
Software/Hardware: Adobe Photoshop, Quark XPress, Mac
Paper/Materials: Raffia, Leaves, Rubber Stamps

Asher Studio

0076
Art Director: Connie Asher
Designers: Russ Chilcoat, Gretchen Wilis
Client: Asher Studio

Software/Hardware: Quark Xpress, Adobe Illustrator, Adobe Photoshop
Paper/Materials: Fox River Confetti, Mohawk Options

b

Bah! Design

0397
Art Director: Neely Ashmun
Designer: Scott Herron
Client: Bah! Design
Software/Hardware: Adobe Illustrator
Paper/Materials: Color Laser Print

0571
Art Director: Neely Ashmun
Designers: Scott Herron, Rob Seale
Client: American Advertising Federation, District Ten
Software/Hardware: Adobe Photoshop, Quark XPress
Paper/Materials: Classic Laid

0608
Art Director: Neely Ashmun
Designers: Scott Herron, Lindsey Taylor
Client: Women & Their Work
Software/Hardware: Adobe Illustrator, Streamline
Paper/Materials: Carnival Yellow

0649
Art Director: Neely Ashmun
Designers: Scott Herron, Rob Seale
Client: Women & Their Work
Software/Hardware: Adobe Photoshop, Quark Xpress

0665
Art Director: Neely Ashmaun
Designer: Scott Herron
Client: Austin Shakespeare Festival
Software/Hardware: Adobe Photoshop, Quark Xpress

0727
Art Director: Neely Ashmun
Designer: Scott Herron
Client: Gwynn David Media Endowment at VT
Software/Hardware: Adobe Illustrator
Paper/Materials: Unisource

0717
Art Director: Neely Ashmun
Designer: Scott Herron
Client: Women & Their Work

Software/Hardware: Adobe Photoshop,
Quark XPress
Paper/Materials: Confetti

0755

Art Director: Neely Ashmun
Designers: Scott Herron, Rob Seale
Client: Austin Shakespeare Festival
Software/Hardware: Adobe Photoshop,
Quark XPress
Paper/Materials: Strathmore Pastel with
Decal Edge

Bandujo, Donker & Brothers

0381

Art Director: Bob Brothers
Designers: Laura Astuto, Anne Dennis
Client: Bank of America

0526

Art Director: Robert Brothers, Jr.
Designer: Carrie Dennis
Client: Susan G. Komen Breast Cancer
Foundation

0865

Art Director: Robert Brothers, Jr.
Designer: Connie Dennis
Client: Juvenile Bipolar Research
Foundation

0731

Art Director: Robert Brothers, Jr.
Designer: Laum Astuto
Client: Make-A-Wish Foundation-NJ

Barbara Brown Marketing & Design

0780

Art Director: Barbara Brown
Designer: Alicia Hoskins
Client: Alzheimers Association
Software/Hardware: Quark XPress, Mac
Paper/Materials: Proterra, Sundance,
Glama Natural

0700

Art Director: Barbara Brown
Designer: Alicia Hoskins
Client: RRPLF
Software/Hardware: Quark XPress, Mac
Paper/Materials: Starwhite Hi-Tech,
Tiara

0843

Art Director: Barbara Brown
Designer: Alicia Hoskins
Client: VCMRF
Software/Hardware: Quark XPress, Mac

Paper/Materials: French Paper

0773

Art Director: Barbara Brown
Designer: Jon A. Leslie
Client: Santa Barbara Museum of Art
Software/Hardware: Quark XPress, Mac
Paper/Materials: Sappi, Glama Natural

0775

Art Director: Barbara Brown
Designer: Jon A. Leslie
Client: RRPLF
Software/Hardware: Quark XPress, Mac
Paper/Materials: Hillsdale

0836

Art Director: Barbara Brown
Designer: Carole Brooks
Client: VCMRF
Software/Hardware: Quark XPress, Mac
Paper/Materials: Precision, Glama-
Natural

Baumann & Baumann

0882

Art Directors: Barbara & Geid Baumann
Designers: Barbara & Geid Baumann
Client: Brandenburg
Software/Hardware: Macromedia
Freehand 10
Paper/Materials: Chromolux 700 350g

0910

Art Directors: Barbara & Geid Baumann
Designers: Barbara & Geid Baumann
Client: Auer & Weber, Muchen Slgt.
Software/Hardware: Macromedia
Freehand 10.0, Adobe Photoshop 6.0
Paper/Materials: Chromolux 700/350g

0914

Art Directors: Barbara & Geid Baumann
Designers: Barbara & Geid Baumann
Client: Baumann & Baumann
Software/Hardware: Macromedia
Freehand
Paper/Materials: Chromolux 700 350g

0912

Art Directors: Barbara & Geid Baumann
Designers: Barbara & Geid Baumann
Client: R & W Dental Technik,
Schwabisch Gmund
Software/Hardware: Macromedia
Freehand 10.0
Paper/Materials: Chromolux 300g

0918

Art Directors: Barbara & Geid Baumann
Designers: Barbara & Geid Baumann
Client: Siemens AG, Munchen
Software/Hardware: Macromedia
Freehand, Adobe Photoshop
Paper/Materials: Chromolux 700/350g

0921

Art Directors: Barbara & Geid Baumann
Designers: Barbara & Geid Baumann
Client: Veischiedene Projecpete
Software/Hardware: Corel Draw,
Pagemaker
Paper/Materials: Naturpapier

0946

Art Directors: Barbara & Geid Baumann
Designers: Barbara & Geid Baumann
Client: Kauffmann, Theilig & Partner
Software/Hardware: Macromedia
Freehand 10
Paper/Materials: Chromolux 700, 300g

0961

Art Directors: Barbara & Geid Baumann
Designers: Barbara & Geid Baumann
Client: Bundesjag Bonn
Software/Hardware: Corel Draw
Paper/Materials: Naturpapier

0996

Art Directors: Barbara & Geid Baumann
Designers: Barbara & Geid Baumann
Client: Lamperte & Sudiow
Software/Hardware: Macromedia
Freehand
Paper/Materials: ProfiSilk 350g

Bear Brook Design

0131

Art Director: Eileen MacAvery Kane
Designers: Amanda Whelen, Niko
Niarhos
Client: Bear Brook Design
Software/Hardware: Mac, Adobe
Photoshop, Adobe Illustrator, Quark
XPress
Paper/Materials: Label Stock, 80 lb.
Silk Text

Becker Design

0706

Designer: Neil Becker
Client: Neil & Amy Becker
Software/Hardware: Quark XPress

Paper/Materials: Mohawk, Superfine
100#C, Soft White, Eggshell Finish,
Glama Natural 27#, Pastel Yellow

0859

Art Director: Neil Becker
Designer: Kaytee Mosher
Client: Garbs
Software/Hardware: Quark XPress,
Adobe Photoshop, Adobe Illustrator
Paper/Materials: 2 Spot PMS Metallic on
Coated Stock, Translucent Envelope

Be Design

0416

Art Director: Eric Read
Designer: Eric Read
Client: Deborah Read
Software/Hardware: Adobe Illustrator
Paper/Materials: Strathmore

0907

Art Director: Eric Read
Designer: Eric Read
Client: Deborah Read
Software/Hardware: Adobe
Paper/Materials: Strathmore

Bekaert & Leroy

0083, 0146, 0157, 0332, 0364, 0365, 0366,
0419, 0434, 0646
Art Director: Johnny Bekaert
Designer: Johnny Bekaert
Client: Kartoen Fabriek
Software/Hardware: Quark XPress,
Adobe Photoshop

Big I Ranch Design Studio

0629

Art Director: Irasema Rivera
Designer: Irasema Rivera
Client: Latina Magazine
Software/Hardware: Quark XPress,
Adobe Illustrator, Mac

Blackbird Creative Services

0485

Designer: Rosemary Campion
Client: Manhattanville College
Software/Hardware: Quark XPress, Mac
Paper/Materials: Coated Cover

BLACKCOFFEE

0046
Art Directors: Mark Gallagher,Laura Savard
Designers: Mark Gallagher, Laura Savard
Client: BLACKCOFFEE
Software/Hardware: Adobe Photoshop, Adobe Illustrator
Paper/Materials: Curious Paper Metallic Ionised Cover

0053
Art Director: Mark Gallagher
Designers: Mark Gallagher, Laura Savard
Client: BLACKCOFFEE
Software/Hardware: Adobe Photoshop, Adobe Illustrator
Paper/Materials: Card-Coated White Cover
Env – Clear Plastic Envelope with Hang Tab

0247
Art Director: Laura Savard
Designers: Mark Gallagher, Laura Savard
Client: Massachusetts General Hospital
Software/Hardware: Adobe Illustrator, Mac
Paper/Materials: Card-Neenah Classic Columns Windsor Blue/Avalanche White 120# Duplex Cover, Envelope-Neenah Classic Columns Avalanche White

0877
Art Directors: Mark Gallagher & Laura Savard
Designers: Mark Gallagher & Laura Savard
Client: BLACKCOFFEE
Software/Hardware: Adobe Illustrator, Mac
Paper/Materials: Burlap Sack, Silver Grommets, Twine

0896
Art Directors: Mark Gallagher & Laura Savard
Designers: Mark Gallagher & Laura Savard
Client: BLACKCOFFEE
Software/Hardware: Adobe Illustrator, Mac
Paper/Materials: Aluminum Tin

BLANK, Inc.

0101
Art Director: Robert Kent Wilson
Designer: Danielle Willis
Client: Number Six Softwave
Software/Hardware: Adobe Illustrator, Mac G4
Paper/Materials: Finch Fine

0451
Art Director: Robert Kent Wilson
Designer: Danielle Willis
Client: Mackerel Sky Architecture
Software/Hardware: Adobe Illustrator, Mac G4
Paper/Materials: Productolith

0501
Art Director: Robert Kent Wilson
Designer: Robert Kent Wilson
Client: Ryan & Martha Wilson
Software/Hardware: Quark XPress, Mac G4
Paper/Materials: Productolith Dull

0569
Art Director: Robert Kent Wilson
Designer: Christine Dzieciolowski
Client: Kickok Warner Cole Architects
Software/Hardware: Adobe Illustrator, Adobe Photoshop, Mac G4
Paper/Materials: Classic Columns

0941
Art Director: Robert Kent Wilson
Designer: Robert Kent Wilson, Danielle Willis, Christine Oziecholowski
Client: BLANK, Inc.
Software/Hardware: Quark XPress, Adobe Illustrator, Adobe Photoshop, Mac
Paper/Materials: Miscellaneous

Blue Inc.

0110
Art Director: Doreen Maddox
Designer: Nina Max Daly
Client: Self-Promotion
Software/Hardware: Mac, Quark XPress, Adobe Illustrator

0691
Art Director: Doreen Maddox
Designer: Tracey Chiang
Client: Self-Promotion
Software/Hardware: Mac, Quark XPress, Adobe Illustrator

Paper/Materials: 100# McCoy Matte Cover, 4 cp & Matte Aqueous Coating

0814
Art Director: Doreen Maddox
Designer: Tracey Chiang
Client: Winston Preparatory School
Software/Hardware: Mac, Quark XPress, Adobe Illustrator
Paper/Materials: Colors Brights 24#, Envelope-Orange, 4cp Vellum Overlay, Solution White 80# Cover Uncoated

0868
Art Director: Doreen Maddox
Designers: Tracey Chiang, Nina Max Daly
Client: Winston Preparatory School
Software/Hardware: Quark XPress, Mac, Adobe Illustrator
Paper/Materials: 80# Porcelain Gloss Cover, PMS Silver & PMS 877 Red with Gloss Aqueous Coating-Envelope-Tuxedo Park White, 4-Bar

0852
Art Director: Doreen Maddox
Designer: Tracey Chiang
Client: Self-Promotion
Software/Hardware: Mac, Quark XPress, Adobe Illustrator
Paper/Materials: Starwhite Vicksburg 130# Cover, Strathmore Bright White 24#

0962
Art Director: Doreen Maddox
Designer: Tracey Chiang
Client: Self-Promotion
Software/Hardware: Mac, Quark XPress, Adobe Illustrator
Paper/Materials: Cotton T-Shirt with Blue Logo, Correspondence Kit (Set of 4 Original Postcards & Blue Inc. Pen, Blue Candle, Kraft paper Bag w/Ribbon & Blue Inc. Hang Tag

0984
Art Director: Doreen Maddox
Designer: Tracey Chiang
Client: Self-Promotion
Software/Hardware: Mac, Quark XPress, Adobe Illustrator
Paper/Materials: Glasses with Invitational Graphics, Mints in Stainless Tin with Corporate Logo, Letterpress Coasters with Invitational Graphics, "Blue Rock" Candy packaging with

Rocks (Chocolate) Packaged in a Kraft Paper Bag, Ribbon & Tag

Bob's Your Uncle

0006, 0008, 0055, 0056, 0082, 0085, 0086, 0089, 0099, 0120, 0121, 0122, 0123, 0165, 0166, 0167, 0168, 0218, 0221, 0234, 0235, 0236, 0238, 0331, 0333
Designer: Martin Yeeles
Software/Hardware: Quark XPress, Mac
Paper/Materials: Gilbert Realm

Boelts/Stratford Associates

0668
Art Directors: Jackson Boelts, Kerry Stratford
Designer: Jennifer Jennings
Client: AZ Council for CASA
Software/Hardware: Macromedia Freehand

0932
Art Directors: Kerry Stratford, Jackson Boelts
Designer: Travis Owens
Client: Southern AZ Aids Foundation
Software/Hardware: Macromedia Freehand

Brauer Design Inc.

0140
Art Director: Bruce Erik Brauer
Designer: Bruce Erik Brauer
Client: WNBC-TV
Software/Hardware: Adobe Illustrator 10
Paper/Materials: Vellum, Silver Elastic

Brookline Street Design, Ltd.

0125
Art Director: Heather Snyder Quinn
Designer: Heather Snyder Quinn
Client: Heather Snyder Quinn
Software/Hardware: Adobe Illustrator, Quark XPress, Mac, Adobe Photoshop
Paper/Materials: Magnet Paper, Mohawk Superfine Soft White

0156
Art Director: Heather Snyder Quinn
Designer: Heather Snyder Quinn
Client: Jen Grochowalski
Software/Hardware: Adobe Illustrator, Adobe Photoshop
Paper/Materials: Photo by Photojenic Photography, Vellum Cover Stock

0164
Art Director: Heather Snyder Quinn
Designer: Heather Snyder Quinn
Client: Jeff, Kris, & Ava

0258, 0468, 0654
Art Director: Heather Snyder Quinn
Designer: Heather Snyder Quinn

0376
Art Director: Heather Snyder Quinn
Designer: Heather Snyder Quinn
Client: McDevitt Family
Software/Hardware: Adobe Photoshop,
Adobe Illustrator
Paper/Materials: Mohawk Superfine

0475
Art Director: Heather Snyder Quinn
Designer: Heather Snyder Quinn
Client: Heather Snyder Quinn
Software/Hardware: Quark XPress
Paper/Materials: Rice Paper, Ribbon

0633
Art Director: Heather Snyder Quinn
Designer: Heather Snyder Quinn
Client: Aimee Calton
Software/Hardware: Quark XPress
Paper/Materials: Mohawk Paper, Ribbon,
Vellum

0672
Art Director: Heather Snyder Quinn
Designer: Heather Snyder Quinn
Client: Susan Kilroy

0683
Art Director: Heather Snyder Quinn
Designer: Heather Snyder Quinn
Client: Kristin Casey
Software/Hardware: Adobe Photoshop,
Adobe Illustrator, Mac
Paper/Materials: Mohawk

0723
Art Director: Heather Snyder Quinn
Designer: Heather Snyder Quinn
Client: Heather Snyder

0676
Art Director: Heather Snyder Quinn
Designer: Heather Snyder Quinn
Client: Jennifer Novak
Software/Hardware: Pencil, Adobe
Photoshop, Mac, Adobe Illustrator
Paper/Materials: Mohawk Superfine

0722
Art Director: Heather Snyder Quinn
Designer: Heather Snyder Quinn

Client: Jessica Winn

0813
Art Director: Heather Snyder Quinn
Designer: Heather Snyder Quinn
Client: Jennifer Grochowalski

0823
Art Director: Heather Snyder Quinn
Designer: Heather Snyder Quinn
Client: Jeanna Berman
Software/Hardware: Mac, Adobe
Photoshop, Adobe Illustrator
Paper/Materials: Strathmore Pastelle,
Mam Image Owned by Bride

0786
Art Director: Heather Snyder Quinn
Designer: Heather Snyder Quinn
Client: Ana Davis
Software/Hardware: Adobe Photoshop,
Adobe Illustrator, Mac
Paper/Materials: Strathmore Pastelle,
Image Copyright DeCordova Museum

0792
Art Director: Heather Snyder Quinn
Designer: Heather Snyder Quinn
Client: Audrey Coyle
Software/Hardware: Adobe Photoshop,
Adobe Illustrator
Paper/Materials: Pencil, Brockaway
Natural Image Provided by Bride,
Unknown Source

0794
Art Director: Heather Snyder Quinn
Designer: Heather Snyder Quinn
Client: Andrea Letourneau
Software/Hardware: Adobe Photoshop,
Adobe Illustrator, Mac
Paper/Materials: Granna Grosso

0809
Art Director: Heather Snyder Quinn
Designer: Heather Snyder Quinn
Client: Jen Grochowalski

0811
Art Director: Heather Snyder Quinn
Designer: Heather Snyder Quinn
Client: Kathryn James

0712
Art Director: Heather Snyder Quinn
Designer: Heather Snyder Quinn
Client: Ellen Hanson
Software/Hardware: Adobe Illustrator,
Mac, Adobe Photoshop
Paper/Materials: Glue, Tape, Bier

Paper, Neenah Classic Laid Vellum
Packets, Flower Seeds

Bruketa & Zinic

0867
Art Directors: Davor Bruketa &
Nikola Zinic
Designers: Davor Bruketa & Nikola Zinic
Client: Rina Penavic
Software/Hardware: Mac
Paper/Materials: Agripina

0998
Art Directors: Davor Bruketa, Nikola
Zinic
Designers: Davor Bruketa, Nikola Zinic
Client: Bruketa & Zinic
Software/Hardware: Mac

Burgard Design

0426
Art Director: Todd Burgard
Designer: Todd Burgard
Client: Todd & Gina Burgard
Software/Hardware: Quark XPress,
Adobe Illustrator, Adobe Photoshop,
Streamline
Paper/Materials: Productolith Dull,
80# 2-Color, 1 side, PMS7436 Purple
& Black

Burgeff Co.

0870
Art Director: Patrick Burgeff
Designer: Patrick Burgeff
Client: Assoc. Mexicana de Orquideas
Software/Hardware: Macromedia
Freehand, Adobe Photoshop
Paper/Materials: Couche Paper, Offset

0913
Art Director: Patrick Burgeff
Designer: Patrick Burgeff
Client: Burgeff Co.
Software/Hardware: Macromedia
Freehand, Adobe Photoshop
Paper/Materials: Sulfated Carton, Offset

0992
Art Director: Patrick Burgeff
Designer: Patrick Burgeff
Client: Guia de Disetro Mexicano
Software/Hardware: Macromedia
Freehand 9.0
Paper/Materials: Sulfate Certon/Offset

C

Cahan & Associates

0804
Art Director: Bill Cahan
Designer: Gary Williams
Client: Zoe

Cahoots

0541
Art Director: Carol Lasky
Designer: Kerri Bennett
Client: Wheelock College
Software/Hardware: Quark XPress, Mac

0694
Art Director: Carol Lasky
Designer: Michael Bouchard
Client: WBUR
Software/Hardware: Adobe Illustrator,
Quark XPress, Adobe Photoshop
Paper/Materials: Sappi, McCoy

Capers Cleveland Design

0477
Art Director: Jenny Daughters-McLain
Designer: Jenny Daughters-McLain
Client: Jenny Daughters & Colin McLain
Software/Hardware: Quark XPress,
Mac G3

Carolynn DeCillo

0022, 0102, 0498
Art Director: Design
Designer: Design
Client: Carolynn DeCillo
Software/Hardware: Quark XPress, Mac
Paper/Materials: Laser Paper

Cave Images, Inc

0430
Art Director: Matt Cave
Designer: Matt Cave
Client: Cave Family
Software/Hardware: Adobe Photoshop,
Quark XPress, Mac
Paper/Materials: Card Stock & Photo

0446
Art Director: Matt Cave
Designer: Matt Cave
Client: Cave Family

Software/Hardware: Adobe Photoshop,
Quark XPress, Mac
Paper/Materials: Curious Iridescent,
Curious Translucent

0459
Art Director: David Edmundson
Designer: David Edmundson
Client: Edmundson Family
Software/Hardware: Adobe Photoshop,
Quark XPress, Mac
Paper/Materials: Cover-Plastic Folders,
Paper-Xerox Paper

0478
Art Director: Matt Cave
Designer: Matt Cave
Client: Cave Family
Software/Hardware: Adobe Photoshop,
Adobe Illustrator, Quark XPress, Mac
Paper/Materials: Card Stock

CC Graphic Design

0124
Art Director: Carolyn Crowley
Designer: Carolyn Crowley
Software/Hardware: Adobe Illustrator,
Mac
Paper/Materials: Chartham Translucent
40# Clear, Stardream Quartz Cover,
Cupiola Italian Paperclips

Chen Design Associates

0802
Art Director: Joshua C. Chen
Designer: Max Spector
Client: Chen Design Associates
Software/Hardware: Adobe Illustrator,
Mac 64
Paper/Materials: Starwhite Vicksburg

0890
Art Director: Joshua C. Chen
Designers: Max Spector, Joshua C.
Chen, Kathryn Hoffman
Client: Chen Design Associates
Software/Hardware: Quark XPress,
Adobe Illustrator, Mac 64
Paper/Materials: Mohawk Superfine
160 #C

Chermayeff & Geismar, Inc.

0881
Art Director: Steff Geissbuhler
Designer: Ian Perkins

Client: Chermayeff & Geismar
Software/Hardware: Adobe Photoshop

Choplogic

0016
Art Director: Walter McCord
Designer: Walter McCord
Client: Choplogic
Software/Hardware: Quark Xpress
Paper/Materials: Mohawk Superfine

0048
Art Director: Walter McCord
Designer: Walter McCord
Client: Langsford Center
Software/Hardware: Quark XPress
Paper/Materials: Mead Mark V

0108
Art Director: Walter McCord
Designer: Walter McCord
Client: Kathy Cary
Paper/Materials: Starwhite Vicksburg

0208
Art Director: Walter McCord
Designer: Walter McCord
Client: Choplogic
Software/Hardware: Quark XPress
Paper/Materials: Champion Kromekote

Christina Blankenship

0613
Art Director: Christina Blankenship
Designer: Christina Blankenship
Client: Christina Blankenship
Software/Hardware: Engraving, Litho,
Quark XPress
Paper/Materials: Evanescent, Curious
and Stardream Paper

Ciro Design

0747
Art Director: Joan Jung
Designer: Katrina Luong
Client: IDSA (Industrial Design Society)
Software/Hardware: Adobe Illustrator
Paper/Materials: Beckett Expressions
"Eucalyptus"

Citron Vert

0289
Art Director: Corinne Fare
Designer: Francois Gervais

Client: Beauté Prestige International
Paper/Materials: Silkscreen Paper

Clearboxx Creative Studio

0388
Art Director: Holli Conger
Designer: Holli Conger
Client: Self-Promo
Software/Hardware: Adobe Illustrator
10, Mac
Paper/Materials: Color Lasers Mounted
on Hand Cut Poster Board

Communication By Design

0533
Art Director: Geoff Aldridge
Designer: Kin Cheung
Client: Communication By Design
Software/Hardware: Illustrator 9.0,
Photoshop 7.0, Quark XPress 4.0
(Apple Mac Platform)
Paper/Materials: 7 Colour Silkscreen
on mark resistant PVC, 3 Colour litho
printing on Colourplan with "Brocade"
embossed surface, Wax seal stamp

Concrete, Chicago

0344
Art Director: Jilly Simons
Designers: Jilly Simons, Regan Todd
Client: Concrete, Chicago
Software/Hardware: Quark Xpress, Mac
OS 9.1
Paper/Materials: Mohawk Superfine,
White Eggshell 100# Cover

0757
Art Director: Jilly Simons
Designers: Jilly Simons, Regan Todd
Client: Washington University in St.
Louis School of Architecture
Software/Hardware: Quark XPress, Mac
OS 9.1
Paper/Materials: Finch Fine, Bright
White, 80# Cover

0866
Art Director: Jilly Simons
Designers: Jilly Simons, Regan Todd
Client: Lookingglass Theatre
Software/Hardware: Quark XPress, Mac
OS 9.1
Paper/Materials: Finch Fine, Bright
White, 80# Cover

d

Dairy

**0009, 0190, 0219, 0220, 0222, 0223, 0280,
0281, 0282, 0283, 0284, 0285, 0286, 0287,
0324, 0384, 0385, 0386, 0399**
Client: Dairy
Software/Hardware: Quark Xpress

0259
Paper/Materials: Paper Bag, Vellum

Damion Hickman Design

0026
Designer: Damion Hickman
Client: Damion Hickman
Software/Hardware: Adobe Illustrator

Danielle Willis

0575
Designer: Danielle Willis
Client: Willis/Weller Wedding
Software/Hardware: Adobe Illustrator,
Mac G4
Paper/Materials: Beckett Expression

Daniels Design, Inc.

0029
Art Director: Larry Daniels
Designer: Larry Daniels
Client: Daniels Design
Software/Hardware: Quark XPress, Mac
Paper/Materials: Strathmore Grandee

Dara Turransky Design

0474
Art Director: Dara Turransky
Designer: Dara Turransky
Client: Emma Wilson
Software/Hardware: Mac, Adobe
Illustrator, Adobe Photoshop
Paper/Materials: French Construction
Kraft Classic Crest Natural White Epson
Heavy Weight Paper

David Carter Design

0077
Art Director: Ashley Barron Mattocks
Designer: Rachel Graham
Client: David Carter Design

Software/Hardware: Adobe Illustrator,
Quark XPress, Mac
Paper/Materials: Phoenix Motion

0486
Art Director: Ashley Barron Mattocks
Designer: Donna Aldredge
Client: David Carter Design
Software/Hardware: Adobe Illustrator,
Quark XPress, Mac
Paper/Materials: Astrolite, Classic Crest,
Classic Laid

David Clark Design

0014, 0363
Designer: David Clark
Client: David Clark Design
Software/Hardware: Adobe Illustrator,
Adobe Photoshop

David Salafia/Laura Farr

0486
Designers: David Salafia, Laura Farr
Client: David Salafia, Laura Farr
Software/Hardware: Quark XPress 4.0
Paper/Materials: Monadnock Dulcet
80# Cover

DC Design

0966
Designer: David Cater

Design 5

0445
Art Director: Ron Nikkel
Designer: Ron Nikkel
Client: Todd & Betsy Pigott
Software/Hardware: Adobe Illustrator,
Mac
Paper/Materials: Classic Crest

0556
Art Director: Ron Nikkel
Designer: Rachel Acton
Client: Fresno Surgery Center
Software/Hardware: Adobe Illustrator,
Mac

0537
Art Director: Ron Nikkel
Designer: Ron Nikkel
Client: Gottschalkes
Software/Hardware: Adobe Illustrator,
Mac

0563
Art Director: Ron Nikkel
Designer: Ron Nikkel
Client: Buddy Systems
Software/Hardware: Adobe Illustrator,
Mac

0728
Art Director: Ron Nikkel
Designer: Tessa Schafer
Client: United Way
Software/Hardware Adobe Illustrator,
Mac
Paper/Materials: Classic Crest

0788
Art Director: Ron Nikkel
Designer: Ron Nikkel
Client: Fresno Advertising Federation
Software/Hardware: Adobe Illustrator,
Mac

0753
Art Director: Ron Nikkel
Designer: Chris DuBurg
Client: United Way
Software/Hardware: Adobe Illustrator,
Mac

0768
Art Director: Ron Nikkel
Designer: Chris DuBurg
Client: Fresno Ad Federation
Software/Hardware: Adobe Illustrator,
Mac

Design Center

0133
Art Director: Cory Docken
Designer: Cory Docken
Client: Design Center
Software/Hardware: Macromedia
Freehand

Design Dairy

0143
Designer: H. Locascio
Client: Joyce Eliason
Software/Hardware: Quark Xpress

0191
Art Director: H. Locascio
Designer: Joyce Eliason

0278
Designer: H. Locascio
Client: Humble Journey

Software/Hardware: Quark XPress
Paper/Materials: Paper, Card

0291
Designer: H. Locascio
Client: Joyce Eliason

0351
Designer: H. Locascio
Client: Shana Goldberg-Meehan
Software/Hardware: Quark XPress

0391
Designer: H. Locascio
Client: Jacki Terrell

0566
Designer: H. Locascio
Client: Carri Levin
Software/Hardware: Quark XPress
Paper/Materials: Card Stock, Matches

0619
Designer: H. Locascio
Client: Stavros

0495
Designer: H. Locascio
Client: Carri Levin
Software/Hardware: Quark XPress
Paper/Materials: Linen

d/g brussels

0407
Art Director: Brigitte Evrard
Designer: Sally Orr
Client: d/g brussels
Software/Hardware: Adobe Illustrator
Paper/Materials: Modigliani Zulu women
Bead-Working

Dig Design

0252
Art Director: Leslie Baker
Designer: Amy Decker
Client: Greenstreet Press
Software/Hardware: Adobe Illustrator
Paper/Materials: Kromkote Glass

Donegan Creative

0661
Designer: Lorraine Donegan
Client: Greg & Beckie Higgins
Software/Hardware: Mac, Quark XPress,
Adobe Illustrator, Adobe Photoshop
Paper/Materials: Japanese Rice
Paper, Ivory Linen Cover, Ivory Linen
Envelopes, Silk Ribbon

Double Happiness Design

0489
Designer: Adrienne Wong

DR2

0326
Art Director: Steven D. Fleshman
Designer: Steven D. Fleshman
Client: DR2
Software/Hardware: Adobe Photoshop,
Quark XPress, Mac
Paper/Materials: Courgar Opaque Cover,
Paperboard Box, Ribbon, Bell

e

Eastern Edge Media Group

0905
Art Director: M. J. Pressley-Jones
Designer: M. J. Pressley-Jones
Client: Eastern Edge Media Group
Software/Hardware: Quark Xpress,
Adobe Photoshop
Paper/Materials: Cambric Beckett White
100# Cover

Ecrie

0468, 0715, 0718, 0829
Art Director: Camilla Sorenson
Client: Private (or Person on Invite)

0531, 0772, 0841
Art Director: Camilla Sorenson
Designer: Camilla Sorenson

Egg Creatives

0003
Art Director: Jason Chen
Designer: Jason Chen
Client: Rhea Consulting
Software/Hardware: Macromedia
Freehand 10
Paper/Materials: Simli

0228
Art Director: Kevin Lee
Designer: Kevin Lee
Client: Egg Creatives
Software/Hardware: Macromedia
Freehand 10, Adobe Photoshop 6.0
Paper/Materials: Keay Kolor, White Gold

0249
Art Director: Jason Chen

Designer: Lim Choon Pin
Client: Egg Creatives
Software/Hardware: Macromedia
Freehand 9.0
Paper/Materials: Art Card & Styrene

0370
Art Director: Jason Chen
Designer: Jason Chen
Client: Egg Creatives
Software/Hardware: Macromedia
Freehand 10
Paper/Materials: Cryogen White

0423
Art Director: Jason Chen
Designer: Jason Chen
Client: Egg Creatives
Software/Hardware: Adobe Photoshop
6.0, Macromedia Freehand 9.0
Paper/Materials: Beckett Enhance

0442
Art Director: Jason Chen
Designer: Jason Chen
Client: Egg Creatives
Software/Hardware: Adobe Photoshop
6.0, Macromedia Freehand 9.0
Paper/Materials: Rives Tradition

0521
Art Director: Jason Chen
Designer: Jason Chen
Client: Warren & Janice
Software/Hardware: Adobe Photoshop
6.0, Macromedia Freehand 9.0
Paper/Materials: Rives Design

0607
Art Director: Jason Chen Y.Z.
Designer: Jason Chen Y.Z.
Client: TD Fabrics PTE Ltd.
Software/Hardware: Macromedia 10
Paper/Materials: 250 gsm Curious
Metallics, Keay Colour Galvanized

0631
Art Director: Jason Chen
Designer: Jason Chen
Client: Singapore Academy of Law
Software/Hardware: Macromedia
Freehand 10
Paper/Materials: Conqueror Dapple
Cream 250 gsm

0679
Art Director: Jason Chen
Designer: Lim Choon Pin
Client: Adrian Khoo & Jeraena
Software/Hardware: Adobe Photoshop,

Macromedia Freehand 10
Paper/Materials: Conqueror Iridescent
Silica Blue 250 gsm

0933
Art Director: Jason Chen
Designer: Jason Chen
Client: Egg Creatives
Software/Hardware: Macromedia
Freehand 10
Paper/Materials: Miscellaneous

Emery Vincent Design

0340
Art Director: Emery Vincent Design
Designer: Emery Vincent Design
Client: Emery Vincent Design
Software/Hardware: Mac, Adobe
Illustrator
Paper/Materials: 200 gsm

0553
Art Director: Emery Vincent Design
Designer: Emery Vincent
Client: IMROC
Software/Hardware: Mac , Adobe
Illustrator
Paper/Materials: 300 gsm Nordset

0973
Art Director: Emery Vincent Design
Designer: Emery Vincent Design
Client: Airport Link
Software/Hardware: Mac, Adobe
Illustrator
Paper/Materials: 260 gsm Snowboard

Emma Wilson Design Company

0473
Designer: Emma Wilson
Client: Emma Wilson
Software/Hardware: Mac OS10,
Macromedia Freehand
Paper/Materials: Vellem Envelope, Fox
River Confetti Card Stock, Paper, Ink
Jet-Printed

0513
Designer: Emma Wilson
Client: The Vine Building LLC
Software/Hardware: Mac OS9,
Macromedia Freehand 9.0
Paper/Materials: On Demand Printing
on 80#c, Vellum Envelope

0500
Designer: Emma Wilson
Client: School of Visual Concepts

Software/Hardware: Mac OS9,
Macromedia Freehand 9.0
Paper/Materials: 80# Gloss Cover On
Demand Printing

0545
Designer: Emma Wilson
Client: Spicers Paper
Software/Hardware: Mac OS9,
Macromedia Freehand 9.0
Paper/Materials: Fraser, Synergy 110
On Demand Printing

0628
Designer: Emma Wilson
Client: Frontier
Software/Hardware: Mac OS9,
Macromedia Freehand
Paper/Materials: 80# Gloss Rouen,
On Demand 4 c Printing

EM Press

0067, 0288
Designer: Elias Roustom

0136
Designers: Elias & Rose Roustom
Software/Hardware: Letterpress
Paper/Materials: Crayon

0539
Designer: Elias Roustom
Client: Letterpress Guild of New England

0856
Designer: Elias Roustom
Client: David Spence

energy energy design

0080, 0087
Art Directors: Jeanette Aramburu,
Stacy Guidice
Designer: Jeanette Aramburu
Client: energy energy design
Software/Hardware: Adobe Illustrator
9.0, Mac
Paper/Materials: Curious Cryogen—
Chartham, Platinum-Envelope

0229
Art Director: Leslie Guidice
Designer: Jeanette Aramburu
Client: energy energy Design
Software/Hardware: Adobe Illustrator
9.0
Paper/Materials: Curious Cryogen-Invite
Wassau-Astrobrite-Envelope

0601
Art Director: Leslie Guidice
Designers: Stacy Guidice & Jeanette
Aramboru
Client: Epic Roots
Software/Hardware: Mac, Adobe
Illustrator 9.0
Paper/Materials: Curious Cryogen,
Invite—Chartham, Platinum, Envelope

0931
Art Director: Leslie Guidice
Designer: Robin Garner
Client: Pal Care
Software/Hardware: Mac, Adobe
Illustrator 9.0
Paper/Materials: Starwhite Vicksburgh

Erin Blankley & Vincent Maccioli

0699
Designer: Erin Blankley
Client: Isabel Pipercic
Software/Hardware: Adobe Illustrator
9.0, Adobe Photoshop
Paper/Materials: Matte Cardstock

España Design

0413
Art Director: Cecilia España
Designer: Cecilia España
Client: Andrea Sevilla
Software/Hardware: Adobe Illustrator

0424
Art Director: Cecilia España
Designer: Cecilia España
Client: Pablo Beretta
Software/Hardware: Adobe Illustrator

f

Factor Design AG

0743
Art Director: Uwe Melichar
Client: Factor Design
Software/Hardware: Macromedia
Freehand, Mac

0805
Art Director: Uwe Melichar
Client: Self Purpose
Software/Hardware: Macromedia
Freehand, Mac

Fern Tiger Associates

0554
Art Director: Fern Tiger
Software/Hardware: Quark XPress, PC

Fiddlesticks Press

0096, 0371, 0372, 0373, 0374, 0375
Designer: Lynn Amft
Software/Hardware: Polymer Plates,
Letterpress
Paper/Materials: Stonehenge Warm
White

Finished Art, Inc

0021
Art Directors: Donna Johnston, Kannex
Fung
Designers: Li-Kim Goh, Marco DiCarlo,
Luis Fernandez
Client: Finished Art, Inc.
Software/Hardware: Adobe Illustrator,
Adobe Photoshop, Traditional
Illustration
Paper/Materials: Gloss Card

0069
Art Directors: Donna Johnston, Kannex
Fung
Designers: Barbara Dorn, Luis
Fernandez, Kannex Funk, Li-Kim Goh,
Mary Jane Hasek, David Lawson,
Rachele Mock, Sutti Sahunalu, Linda
Stuart
Client: Finished Art, Inc.
Software/Hardware: Adobe Illustrator,
Adobe Photoshop, Traditional
Illustration
Paper/Materials: Curious Metallic

Firebelly Design Co.

0163
Art Director: Dawn Hancock
Designer: Mikel Rosenthal
Client: Firebelly Design Co.
Software/Hardware: Adobe Illustrator
9, Mac G4
Paper/Materials: Mohawk Superfine
Smooth 100#C

0686
Art Director: Dawn Hancock
Designer: Dawn Hancock
Client: Neo-Futurists' Theatre
Software/Hardware: Adobe Illustrator
9, Mac G4

0766
Art Director: Dawn Hancock
Designer: Dawn Hancock
Client: Bailiwick Repertory
Software/Hardware: Adobe Illustrator
9, Mac G4

0883
Art Director: Dawn Hancock
Designer: Dawn Hancock
Client: Ladendorf Bros.
Software/Hardware: Adobe Illustrator
9, Mac 64
Paper/Materials: Mohawk Superfine

0942
Art Director: Dawn Hancock
Designer: Mikel Rosenthal
Client: Video Machete
Software/Hardware: Adobe Illustrator
9, Mac 64

0976
Art Director: Dawn Hancock
Designer: Dawn Hancock
Client: Firebelly Design Co.
Software/Hardware: Adobe Illustrator
9, Mac 64
Paper/Materials: French (Various)

Flight Creative

0980
Art Director: Lisa Nankervis
Designers: Lisa Nankervis, Alex Fregon,
Davit Stelma
Client: Flight Creative
Software/Hardware: Adobe Illustrator
9.0, 3D Studio Max
Paper/Materials: Raleigh Sumo
300gsm/200gsm

Form Funf Bremen

0197
Art Director: Daniel Bastian
Fotographer: Daniel Bastian
Client: Form Funf
Software/Hardware: Fotolab
Paper/Materials: Fotoprint B/W

Free Association

0710
Designer: Jason Fairchild
Client: Self
Software/Hardware: XActo/Hands
Paper/Materials: Handmade paper from
Thailand/Japan

g

Garet McIntyre

0518
Client: Garet McIntyre

0744, 0807, 0869
Client: Morning Star Cafe
Software/Hardware: Quark XPress

Garfinkel Design

0741
Art Director: Wendy Garfinkel-Gold
Client: Georgia Museum of Art
Software/Hardware: Quark XPress
4.1, Mac
Paper/Materials: Mohawk Ultrafelt
Softwhite with Deckle, Mohawk
Superfine Softwhite

GARISGRAFIS

0595
Art Director: Mira Melinda
Designer: Liza Zahir
Client: Nana & Novi (Wedding
Invitation)
Paper/Materials: Ivory 320 gr

Gateway Arts

0591
Art Director: Dave Carlson
Designer: Gina Cusano
Client: Amgen
Software/Hardware: Macromedia
Dreamweaver, Adobe Photoshop
Paper/Materials: Online Invite

0851
Art Director: Dave Carlson
Designers: Gina Cusano, Cameron
Smith
Client: Amgen
Software/Hardware: Macromedia
Dreamweaver, Adobe Photoshop
Paper/Materials: Online Invite, Printed

0850
Art Director: Dave Carlson
Designers: Gina Cusano, Cameron
Smith
Client: Wellpoint
Software/Hardware: Macromedia
Dreamweaver, Adobe Illustrator, Adobe
Photoshop

Paper/Materials: Online/100# Gloss
Cover

Gee & Chung Design

0535
Art Director: Earl Gee
Designers: Earl Gee, Fani Chung
Client: DCM-Doll Capital Management
Software/Hardware: Quark XPress,
Adobe Illustrator, Adobe Photoshop,
Apple Power Mac 64
Paper/Materials: Paper: Strathmore
Softwhite Wove 110# Cover
Envelope: 30# Chartham Platinum
Translucent

Gervais

0040, 0189, 0202, 0297, 0298, 0299,
0300, 0383
Art Director: Francois Gervais
Designer: Francois Gervais
Client: Francois Gervais
Software/Hardware: Adobe Photoshop
6.0

Gervais/Citron Vert

0206
Art Director: Gervais/Citron Vert
Designer: Francois Gervais
Client: Beauté Prestige International
Paper/Materials: Fedrigoni

0380
Art Director: Gervais/Citron Vert
Designer: Francois Gervais
Client: Citron Vert Agency
Paper/Materials: Fedrigoni

Get Smart Design Company

0203
Art Director: Tom Culbertson
Designer: GSDC Staff
Client: Get Smart Design Company
Software/Hardware: Macromedia
Freehand
Paper/Materials: Used Christmas
Albums, Vinyl

Goodesign

0514
Art Director: Diane Shaw
Client: KEENA
Software/Hardware: Quark XPress

Paper/Materials: Starwhite Tiara 130lb Cover Letterpress

0771
Art Director: Kathryn Hammill
Client: American Federation of Arts
Software/Hardware: Quark XPress
Paper/Materials: Offset, Studley Press

0616
Designer: Diane Shaw
Client: Rio Rocket Valledor & Diane Shaw
Software/Hardware: Quark XPress
Paper/Materials: Starwhite Tiara 130lb Cover Offset-Corporate Communications

0929
Art Directors: Kathryn Hammill, Diane Shaw
Client: Goodesign
Software/Hardware: Quark XPress, Adobe Illustrator

Grapevine

0577
Art Director: Karen Bartolomei
Designer: Karen Bartolomei
Client: Kristie Dimitriou
Software/Hardware: Adobe Illustrator, Quark XPress, Adobe Photoshop

0674
Art Director: Karen Bartolomei
Designer: Karen Bartolomei
Client: Kathryn McCarthy & Chad Maguire
Software/Hardware: Adobe Illustrator, Quark XPress, Adobe Photoshop

0812
Art Director: Karen Bartolomei
Designer: Karen Bartolomei
Client: Myself & My Husband
Software/Hardware: Adobe Illustrator, Quark XPress, Adobe Photoshop

0815
Art Director: Karen Bartolomei
Designer: Karen Bartolomei
Client: Jennifer & Timm Runion (Couple)
Software/Hardware: Adobe Illustrator, Quark XPress, Adobe Photoshop

0817
Art Director: Karen Barolomei
Designer: Karen Bartolomei
Client: Sharon Foley (Bride)

Software/Hardware: Adobe Illustrator. Quark XPress, Adobe Photoshop

0725
Art Director: Karen Bartolomei
Designer: Karen Bartolomei
Client: Pat Baxter (Her Daughter's Wedding)
Software/Hardware: Adobe Illustrator, Quark XPress, Adobe Photoshop

0787
Art Director: Karen Bartolomei
Designer: Karen Bartolomei
Client: Megan Murphy (Bride)
Software/Hardware: Adobe Illustrator, Quark XPress, Adobe Photoshop

0793
Art Director: Karen Bartolomei
Designer: Karen Bartolomei
Client: Debbie Adners (Step-Mother of Bride)
Software/Hardware: Adobe Illustrator, Quark XPress, Adobe Photoshop

0639
Art Director: Karen Bartolomei
Designer: Karen Bartolomei
Client: Lorie Hamermesh (Mother of Bride)
Software/Hardware: Adobe Illustrator, Quark XPress, Adobe Photoshop

0641
Art Director: Karen Bartolomei
Designer: Karen Bartolomei
Client: Bridget Shea & Carl Lacey
Software/Hardware: Adobe Illustrator, Quark XPress, Adobe Photoshop

0873
Art Director: Karen Bartolomei
Designer: Karen Bartolomei
Client: Nicki Closset (Mother of Bride)
Software/Hardware: Adobe Illustrator, Quark XPress, Adobe Photoshop

0843
Art Director: Karen Bartolomei
Designer: Karen Bartolomei
Client: Liesi Crooker (Bride)
Software/Hardware: Adobe Illustrator, Quark XPress, Adobe Photoshop

0711
Art Director: Karen Bartolomei
Designer: Karen Bartolomei
Client: Diana Tapper (Bride)

Software/Hardware: Adobe Illustrator, Quark XPress, Adobe Photoshop

0985
Art Director: Karen Bartolomei
Designer: Karen Bartolomei
Client: Grapevine
Software/Hardware: Adobe Illustrator, Quark XPress, Adobe Photoshop

Graphic Type Services

0584
Art Director: Ravit Advocat
Designer: Ravit Advocat
Client: Twinings Tea
Software/Hardware: Quark XPress, Adobe Illustrator
Paper/Materials: 4/4 Cream Uncoated

1000
Art Director: Ravit Advocat
Designer: Ravit Advocat
Client: Twinings Tea
Software/Hardware: Quark XPress 4.1, Adobe Photoshop
Paper/Materials: Curious Papers, Iridescent & Confetti, Translucent Envelope, 4/4 Invite & Foil Stamp, Silver on Envelope

graphische formgebung

0084
Art Director: Herbert Rohsiepe
Designer: Herbert Rohsiepe
Client: adesso AG
Software/Hardware: Macromedia Freehand, Mac

0115
Art Director: Herbert Rohsiepe
Designer: Herbert Rohsiepe
Client: wp.DATA
Software/Hardware: Macromedia Freehand, Mac

0107
Art Director: Herbert Rohsiepe
Designer: Herbert Rohsiepe
Client: adesso AG
Software/Hardware: Macromedia Freehand, Mac
Paper/Materials: Lake Paper Motion

0330
Art Director: Herbert Rohsiepe
Designer: Herbert Rohsiepe
Client: AHG AAg

Software/Hardware: Macromedia Freehand, Mac
Paper/Materials: Arjo Wiggins Conqueror

0848, 0540
Art Director: Herbert Rohsiepe
Designer: Herbert Rohsiepe
Client: adesso AG
Software/Hardware: Macromedia Freehand, Mac
Paper/Materials: Arjo Wiggins Conqueror

0853
Art Director: Herbert Rohsiepe
Designer: Herbert Rohsiepe
Client: Prof. Dr. Volker Gruhn, University of Leipzig
Software/Hardware: Macromedia Freehand, Mac
Paper/Materials: Roemerturm Precioso

0947
Designer: Herbert Rohsiepe
Client: graphische formgebung
Software/Hardware: Macromedia Freehand, Mac
Paper/Materials: Roemerturm Phoenixmotion, Arjo Wiggins Impressions

0970
Art Director: Herbert Rohsiepe
Designer: Herbert Rohsiepe
Client: graphische formgebung
Software/Hardware: Macromedia Freehand, Mac
Paper/Materials: Arjo Wiggins Impressions

Greta Berger

0377, 0620, 0621, 0622, 0623, 0624
Designer: Greta Berger
Software/Hardware: Mac, Adobe Illustrator 8.0
Paper/Materials: Benefit 100% Recycled Snow White

Greteman Group

0421
Art Director: James Strange
Designer: James Strange
Client: Cero's Candies
Software/Hardware: Macromedia Freehand

0533
Art Director: Sonia Greteman
Designer: Garrett Fresh

Client: Kitchen & Bath
Software/Hardware: Macromedia
Freehand

0667

Art Directors: Sonia Greteman, James Strange
Designers: James Strange, Garrett Fresh
Client: Connect Care
Software/Hardware: Macromedia Freehand

0729

Art Directors: Garrett Fresh, Sonia Greteman, Craig Tomson
Designer: Garrett Fresh
Client: Connect Care
Software/Hardware: Macromedia Freehand

0863

Art Director: Craig Tomson
Designer: Craig Tomson
Client: Mike Chance
Software/Hardware: Macromedia Freehand, Adobe Photoshop

0874

Art Directors: Sonia Greteman, Craig Tomson
Designer: Craig Tomson
Client: Flexjet
Software/Hardware: Macromedia Freehand
Paper/Materials: Carnival Groove

0894

Art Director: James Strange
Designers: James Strange, Craig Tomson
Client: Greteman Group for Habitat for Humanity
Software/Hardware: Macromedia Freehand

0960

Art Directors: Sonia Greteman, James Strange, Craig Tomson
Designers: James Strange, Craig Tomson
Client: Greteman Group

Group 55 Marketing

0264

Art Director: Jeannette Gutierrez
Designer: Jeannette Gutierrez
Client: Group 55 Marketing
Software/Hardware: Macromedia

Freehand 8.0, Mac
Paper/Materials: HP Deskjet 810 Output

0265

Art Director: Jeannette Gutierrez
Client: Jeannette Gutierrez
Software/Hardware: Macromedia Freehand 8.0, Mac
Paper/Materials: French Construction

0509

Art Director: Courtney Heisel
Designer: Courtney Heisel
Client: Stratford Place Apartments
Software/Hardware: Macromedia Freehand 8.0, Mac
Paper/Materials: 80# Cover DeltaSilk

0861

Art Director: Jeannette Gutierrez
Designer: Jeannette Gutierrez
Client: Store of Dreams
Software/Hardware: Macromedia Freehand 8.0, Mac
Paper/Materials: 14 pt. Tango CZS

0902

Art Director: Jeannette Gutierrez
Designer: Jeannette Gutierrez
Client: Group 55 marketing
Software/Hardware: Macromedia Freehand 8.0, Mac
Paper/Materials: Black & White Laser Output on Fraser Genesis

Gulla Design

0398

Art Director: Steve Gulla
Designer: Steve Gulla
Client: Gulla Design
Software/Hardware: Adobe Illustrator, Mac
Paper/Materials: Coated 18 80lb Cover

0887

Art Director: Steve Gulla
Designer: Steve Gulla
Client: New York University, Office of Career Services
Software/Hardware: Adobe Illustrator, Mac
Paper/Materials: 10 pt. Coated 2 Sides

Gunter Advertising

0503

Art Director: Sarah Grimm
Designer: Sarah Grimm

Client: Gunter Advertising
Software/Hardware: Adobe Photoshop

0512

Art Director: Sarah Grimm
Designer: Sarah Grimm
Client: Gunter Advertising
Software/Hardware: Adobe Illustrator

0580

Art Director: Sarah Grimm
Designer: Sarah Grimm
Client: Gunter Advertising
Software/Hardware: Adobe Illustrator, Adobe Photoshop

0593

Art Director: Bill Patton
Designer: Sarah Grimm
Client: Dean Health Plan
Software/Hardware: InDesign

Gutierrez Design Associates

0735

Art Director: Jeannette Gutierrez
Designer: Jeannette Gutierrez
Client: Ann Arbor Ad Club
Software/Hardware: Macromedia Freehand, Mac
Paper/Materials: Century Gloss

0638, 0657

Art Director: Jeannette Gutierrez
Designer: Jeannette Gutierrez
Client: Automotive News
Software/Hardware: Macromedia Freehand 8.0, Mac
Paper/Materials: Sappi Lustro Gloss

0495

Art Director: Jeannette Gutierrez
Designer: Jeannette Gutierrez
Client: Greening of Detroit
Software/Hardware: Macromedia Freehand 8.0, Mac
Paper/Materials: Sappi Lustro Dull

0959

Art Director: Jeannette Gutierrez
Designer: Jeannette Gutierrez
Client: Jeannette Gutierrez
Software/Hardware: Macromedia Freehand 8.0, Mac
Paper/Materials: Neenah Classic Crest

h

hagopian ink

0126

Art Director: Christina Hagopian
Designer: Christina Hagopian
Client: Hagopian Ink
Software/Hardware: Letterpress
Paper/Materials: Strathmore Pastell, Platen Press 6 X 10, Etching Ink, Die

0301

Art Director: Christina Hagopian
Designer: Christina Hagopian
Client: hagopian ink
Software/Hardware: Adobe Illustrator, Mac
Paper/Materials: Carnival Colors, Summer Eyelet, Wire Ornament Hook, Beach Sand, Laser Printed

0392, 0393, 0394, 0395, 0396

Art Director: Christina Hagopian
Designer: Christina Hagopian
Client: Hagopian Ink
Software/Hardware: Adobe Illustrator
Paper/Materials: Hahnamuhle Copperplate, 1.00gPostcards, 300# (notecards)

Hams Design

0548

Art Director: Bill Hams
Designer: Renee Kae Szajna
Client: Valspar Corporation
Software/Hardware: Adobe Photoshop, Quark XPress
Paper/Materials: Offset Printing, Sappi Strobe Silk 100# Cover, Gold Grommets

Hans Design

0472

Art Director: Bill Hans
Designer: Kristin Miaso
Client: E. Cheval
Software/Hardware: Adobe Illustrator
Paper/Materials: Stardream Envelopes, Handmade Gold Paper, Vellum, French Construction Black, Black Grommets, Raffia Tie

0695

Art Director: Bill Hans
Designer: Kristin Miaso
Client: S. Mack

Software/Hardware: Adobe Illustrator 10,
Paper/Materials: French Construction Plotter Paper

Hecht Design

0044
Art Director: Alice Hecht
Designer: Studio
Client: Hecht Design
Software/Hardware: Adobe Illustrator
Paper/Materials: Paper Coaster with Letterpress

0782
Art Director: Alice Hecht
Designers: Alice Hecht, Elisa Rogers
Client: Austin Architects
Software/Hardware: Quark XPress
Paper/Materials: Mohawk Superfine

0784
Art Director: Alice Hecht
Designers: Alice Hecht, Derek George
Client: UK Architects
Software/Hardware: Quark XPress
Paper/Materials: Mohawk Superfine

0953
Art Director: Alice Hecht
Designers: Elisa Rogers, Megan Verdugo
Client: Hecht Design
Software/Hardware: Adobe Illustrator
Paper/Materials: Glass, Offset Stock

Hoffmann Angelic Design

0079
Art Director: Andrea Hoffmann
Designer: Andrea Hoffmann
Client: Hoffmann Angelic Design
Paper/Materials: Hand-Crafted Metallic Ink, Dimensional Fabric Paint, Hand Lettering, Ivan Angelic

0403
Art Director: Andrea Hoffmann
Designer: Andrea Hoffmann
Client: Hoffmann Angelic Design
Software/Hardware: Adobe Photoshop, Mac
Paper/Materials: Corrugated Board, Adhesive Rhinestone

Hutchinson Associates, Inc.

0292
Art Director: Jerry Hutchinson
Designer: Jerry Hutchinson
Client: Hutchinson Associates
Software/Hardware: Mac, Quark XPress
Paper/Materials: Superfine

0427
Art Director: Jerry Hutchinson
Designer: Jerry Hutchinson
Client: Frankel/Poe
Software/Hardware: Mac, Quark XPress
Paper/Materials: Mohawk Superfine

0542
Art Director: Jerry Hutchinson
Designer: Jerry Hutchinson
Client: Kids for Kids
Software/Hardware: Mac, Quark XPress
Paper/Materials: Mohawk Spetia

i

IC Companys In-house

0254
Art Director: Vibeke Nodskov
Designer: Vibeke Nodskov
Client: IC Companys
Software/Hardware: Adobe Illustrator
Paper/Materials: Macro Gloss 270g

Ideas Frescas

0832
Art Director: Lee Newham
Designer: Lee Newham
Client: Carol Christie
Software/Hardware: Adobe Photoshop, Adobe Illustrator, Mac

IE Design

0343
Art Director: Marcie Carson
Designers: Marcie Carson, Richard Haynie
Client: IE Design
Software/Hardware: Mac, Quark XPress, Adobe Illustrator, Adobe Photoshop

0530
Art Director: Marcie Carson
Designer: Cya Nelson
Client: DaVita
Software/Hardware: Mac, Quark XPress, Adobe Illustrator, Adobe Photoshop

0647
Art Director: Marcie Carson
Designer: Amy Klass

Client: Davita
Software/Hardware: Mac, Quark XPress, Adobe Illustrator, Adobe Photoshop
Paper/Materials: Mohawk 6/6

0855
Art Director: Marcie Carson
Designers: Amy Klass, Cya Nelson
Client: U.S.C. Libraries
Software/Hardware: Mac, Adobe Illustrator, Quark XPress, Adobe Photoshop

0857
Art Director: Marcie Carson
Designer: Cya Nelson
Client: U.S.C. School of Cinema & T.V.
Software/Hardware: Mac, Adobe Illustrator, Adobe Photoshop, Quark XPress
Paper/Materials: Silver, Black & Varnish, 2-Color Foil Stamp

0927
Art Director: Marcie Carson
Designer: Amy Klass
Client: IE Design
Software/Hardware: Mac, Quark Xpress, Adobe Illustrator, Adobe PhotoShop
Paper/Materials: Hanes T, 3 color

Image/Visual Communications

0401
Art Director: Dominick Sarica
Designer: Priska Diaz
Client: New York City College of Technology
Software/Hardware: Mac, Quark XPress, Adobe Photoshop
Paper/Materials: Mohawk Superfine, 65 lb. Ultra White Smooth

Image Zoo

0995
Art Director: Jamie Flint
Designer: Jamie Flint
Client: Arts Council NI
Software/Hardware: Mac, Adobe Photoshop
Paper/Materials: Helo Silk 210 gsm

Indian Hill Press

0015, 0013, 0035, 0036, 0037, 0038, 0130, 0132, 0145, 0146, 0147, 0148, 0167, 0179, 0181, 0204, 0212, 0213, 0214, 0293, 0294, 0295, 0296, 0319, 0320, 0321

Designer: Daniel A. Waters
Client: Indian Hill Press
Software/Hardware: Letterpress
Paper/Materials: Strathmore Pastelle

iNK design

0961
Designers: Wing Ngan, Maggie Cheung
Client: AIGA Boston
Printer: Postcardpress.com

Innova Ideas & Services

0574
Art Directors: Dawn Budd, Linda Griffen
Designer: Jessica Oakland
Client: Rachel Oakland
Software/Hardware: Quark Xpress

INOX Design

0739
Art Director: Creative Team
Designer: Masa Magnoni
Client: Italo & Tecla
Software/Hardware: Adobe Illustrator
Paper/Materials: Paper, Magnet

inpraxis, raum fur gestaitung

0479
Art Directors: A. Kranz & C. Schaffner
Designer: A. Kranz & C. Schaffner
Client: affetti strumentali
Software/Hardware: Quark XPress 4.01, Mac G4
Paper/Materials: 3 Color Offset printing on 240g Coated Stock

0634
Art Directors: A. Kranz & C. Schaffner
Designers: A. Kranz & C. Schaffner
Client: Objektform
Software/Hardware: Quark XPress 4.01, Mac G4
Paper/Materials: 5 Color Offset Printing on 240g Coated Stock

0778
Art Directors: A. Kranz, C. Schaffner
Designers: A. Kranz, C. Schaffner
Client: affetti strumentali
Software/Hardware: Quark XPress 4.0, Mac G4
Paper/Materials: Laser Coy on Different papers

Kehoe & Kehoe Design Associates

0279
Designer: Deborah Kehoe
Client: Kehoe & Kehoe Design Associates

0361
Art Director: Deborah Kehoe
Designer: Deborah Kehoe
Client: Kehoe & Kehoe Design Associates

0408
Designer: Deborah Kehoe
Client: Caroline Crawford

0643
Art Director: Deborah Kehoe
Designer: Lori Myers
Client: Kehoe & Kehoe Design Associates

Kendall Ross

0231
Art Director: David Kendall
Designers: Scott Fricsen, Helen Kong
Client: Kendall Ross
Software/Hardware: Adobe Illustrator, Mac
Paper/Materials: Vintage Velvet 80#C

0506
Art Director: David Kendall
Designer: David Kendall
Client: Bellevue Art Museum
Software/Hardware: Adobe Illustrator
Paper/Materials: Various

0523
Art Director: David Kendall
Designer: Shannon Ecke
Client: Tacoma Art Museum
Software/Hardware: Adobe Illustrator
Paper/Materials: Topkote 80#C

0783
Art Director: David Kendall
Designer: Josh Michas
Client: Tacoma Art Museum
Software/Hardware: Adobe Illustrator
Paper/Materials: Topkote

0991
Art Director: David Kendall
Designer: David Kendall
Client: Tacoma Art Museum
Software/Hardware: Adobe Illustrator
Paper/Materials: Topkote

Kevin Akers Design & Imagery

0356, 0415, 0436
Art Director: Kevin Akers
Designer: Kevin Akers
Client: Kevin & Judee Akers
Software/Hardware: Adobe Illustrator

0420
Art Director: Kevin Akers
Client: Kevin Akers Design & Imagery

0519, 0550, 0749
Art Director: Kevin Akers
Designer: Kevin Akers
Client: Philharmonic Baroque Orchestra

0943
Art Director: Kevin Akers
Client: Burson-Marsteller

0952
Art Director: Kevin Akers
Designer: Various
Client: Performance Printing

Kinetik

0971
Designers: Beth Clawson, Jeff Fabian,
Beverley Hunter, Mike Joosse, Katie
Kroener, Jackie Ratsch, Scott Rier, Sam
Shelton, Jenny Skillman
Client: Mark Finkenstaedt
Software/Hardware: Quark XPress, Mac

0978
Art Directors: Beth Clawson, Jeff
Fabian,
Beverley Hunter, Mike Joosse, Katie
Kroener,
Jackie Ratsch, Scott Rier, Sam Shelton,
Jenny Skillman
Designers: Beth Clawson, Jeff Fabian,
Beverley Hunter, Mike Joosse, Katie
Kroener,
Jackie Ratsch, Scott Rier, Sam Shelton,
Jenny Skillman
Client: Kinetik
Software/Hardware: Quark XPress, Mac

KKargl Graphic Design

0480
Designer: Kathleen W. Kargl
Client: University of Dayton Alumni
House
Software/Hardware: Macromedia
Freehand

0702, 0785
Designer: Kathleen W. Kargl
Client: University of Dayton Rike Center
Gallery
Software/Hardware: Macromedia
Freehand

KO création

0457
Art Director: KO création
Designer: Maxime Levesque
Client: IDX
Software/Hardware: Adobe Illustrator,
Adobe Photoshop
Paper/Materials: Tango 24 pts, Matte
lamination

0625
Art Director: KO création
Designer: Christian Belanger
Client: Chants Libres
Software/Hardware: Adobe Illustrator,
Adobe Photoshop
Paper/Materials: Domtar Luna Cover
100 lbs.

0635
Art Director: Dennis Dulude
Designer: Dennis Dulude
Client: Marie Beaulieu & Mario
Thibodeau
Software/Hardware: Adobe Illustrator
Paper/Materials: Domtar Solutions Cover
80lbs, Domtar Solutions Text 24lbs

0965
Art Director: Annie Lachapelle
Designer: Annie Lachapelle
Client: Christian Guay Photographe
Software/Hardware: Adobe InDesign,
HB Pencil, Right Hand
Paper/Materials: Horizon Silk Cover
100 lbs.

Knezic/Pavone

0440
Art Director: Robinson C. Smith
Designer: Robinson C. Smith
Client: Personal
Software/Hardware: Adobe Illustrator,
Mac

Kolegram Design

0139
Art Director: Mike Teixeira
Designer: Andre Mitchell

Client: Kolegram Design
Software/Hardware: Quark XPress 4.0

0154
Art Director: Mike Teixeira
Designer: Jean-Francois Plante
Client: Kolegram Design
Software/Hardware: Quark XPress 4.0

0516
Art Director: Mike Teixeira
Designer: Annie Tanguay
Client: Tourisme-Outaouais
Software/Hardware: Quark XPress 4.0

0555
Art Director: Mike Teixeira
Designer: Mike Teixeira
Client: Advertising & Design Association
Software/Hardware: Quark XPress 4.0

0673
Art Director: Mike Teixeira
Designers: Annie Tanguay, Gontran
Blais
Client: Kolegram Design
Software/Hardware: Quark XPress 4.0

0726
Art Director: Mike Teixeira
Designer: Jean-Francois Plante
Client: Portrait Gallery of Canada
Software/Hardware: Quark XPress 4.0

0701
Art Director: Mike Teixeira
Designer: Gontran Blais
Client: Buntin Reid Papers
Software/Hardware: Quark XPress 4.0

0919
Art Director: Mike Teixeira
Designer: Mike Teixeira
Client: Kolegram & Headlight Imagery
Software/Hardware: Quark XPress 4.0

0945
Art Director: Mike Teixeira
Designer: Mike Teixeira
Client: Kolegram Design
Software/Hardware: Quark XPress 4.0

Kristina E. Kim

**0255, 0256, 0257, 0273, 0302, 0303,
0304, 0306**
Client: Self-Promotion
Paper/Materials: Handmade Circle,
Square Punches, Scallop Scissors, Fox
River Crushed Leaf poppy Sparkles, 110
lb Cover Plus Curious paper Metallics,

Ice Gold, 93 lb. Cover, Curious paper
Metallics, Gold Leaf 92 lb. Cover, 3M
Foam Tape

Kristin Cullen

0118, 0481
Designer: Kristin Cullen
Software/Hardware: Adobe Illustrator,
Mac
Paper/Materials: French Frostone

0490
Designer: Kristin Cullen
Client: Kelly Ann & Kevin Flynn
Software/Hardware: Quark XPress,
Adobe Illustrator, Adobe Photoshop,
Mac
Paper/Materials: French Frostone,
Glama Natural Vellum

Kristi Norgaard

0551
Client: Norgaard & Terleph

I

Laura McFadden Design, Inc.

0004, 0899
Art Director: Laura McFadden Design,
Inc.
Designer: Laura McFadden Design, Inc.
Client: Laura McFadden
Software/Hardware: Quark XPress, Adobe
Photoshop
Paper/Materials: Paper

Laura Ploszaj

0588
Client: Sara Ploszaj
Software/Hardware: Quark XPress,
Adobe Illustrator
Paper/Materials: Strathmore Writing,
Soft Blue Cover, Letterpress

Leibow Studios

0557
Art Director: Paul Leibow
Designer: Paul Leibow
Client: Polo Gallery
Software/Hardware: Adobe Photoshop,
Quark XPress
Paper/Materials: Coated Card Stock

0690
Art Director: Paul Leibow
Designer: Paul Leibow
Client: The Liquid Gallery
Software/Hardware: Adobe Photoshop,
Quark XPress
Paper/Materials: Coated Card Stock

0748
Art Director: Paul Leibow
Designer: Paul Leibow
Client: Parker Gallery
Software/Hardware: Adobe Photoshop,
Quark XPress
Paper/Materials: Coated Card Stock

0925
Art Director: Paul Leibow
Designer: Paul Leibow
Client: Leibow Studios
Software/Hardware: Adobe Photoshop,
Quark XPress
Paper/Materials: Coated Card Stock

Lemley Design Company

0893
Art Director: David Lemley
Designers: David Lemley, Yuri Shuets
Client: Lemley Design Company
Software/Hardware: Macromedia
Freehand 10
Paper/Materials: White Cover Stock,
Beef Jerky, Vacuum Seal Wrap

0974
Art Director: David Lemley
Designers: David Lemley, Yuri Shuets
Client: Lemley Design Company
Software/Hardware: Macromedia
Freehand 10, Adobe Photoshop 6.0,
Mac 64
Paper/Materials: Neenah Paper, Red
Ribbon, Silver Eyelets

Les Cheneaux Design

0047
Designer: Lori Young
Client: Les Cheneaux Design
Software/Hardware: Mac OS 9.5
Paper/Materials: Silver Painted Card
Stock with Affixed Card

0525
Designer: Lori Young
Client: Ashford Village Block Party
Software/Hardware: Quark XPress 3.3,
Adobe Illustrator 9.0

Paper/Materials: #70 Matte Card Stock

Letter Design

0940
Art Director: Paul Shaw
Designer: Paul Shaw
Client: Paul Shaw
Software/Hardware: Quark XPress, Mac
Paper/Materials: Strathmore Writing

Likovni Studio D.O.O.

0072, 0171
Client: Likovni Studio D.O.O.
Software/Hardware: Macromedia
Freehand, Mac
Paper/Materials: Magnomatt

0515
Client: Archaeological Museum Zagreb
Software/Hardware: Macromedia
Freehand, Mac
Paper/Materials: Magnomatt

Liquid Agency, Inc.

0670
Art Director: Lisa Kliman
Designer: Julia Held
Client: San Jose Downtown Association
Software/Hardware: Quark XPress, Mac

Little Smiles Co.

0098, 0186, 0769
Art Director: Stephanie Zelman
Client: Little Smiles Co.

Lloyds Graphic Design

0456
Art Director: Alexander Lloyd
Designer: Alexander Lloyd
Client: Alexander Lloyd
Software/Hardware: Mac, Macromedia
Freehand, Adobe Photoshop
Paper/Materials: Matt 300 gsm.

0632
Art Director: Alexander Lloyd
Designer: Alexander Lloyd
Client: Marlborough District Council
Software/Hardware: Mac, Macromedia
Freehand
Paper/Materials: Gloss Art 150 gms

0732
Art Director: Alexander Lloyd
Designer: Alexander Lloyd

Client: Bay of Many Coves Resort
Software/Hardware: Mac, Macromedia
Freehand
Paper/Materials: Matt Art 300 gsm

0930
Art Director: Alexander Lloyd
Designer: Alexander Lloyd
Client: Accord Insurance
Software/Hardware: Mac, Macromedia
Freehand, Adobe Photoshop
Paper/Materials: Coated Card Stock

Logica3 Ltd

0041
Art Director: Lisa Page
Designer: Phil Oster
Client: Big Leap Media
Software/Hardware: Quark XPress, Mac
Paper/Materials: Mohawk Superfine,
100# Cover

Loudmouth Graphics

0462
Art Director: David Schroer
Designer: David Schroer
Client: David Schroer, Sue Mullins
Software/Hardware: Mac, Quark XPress,
Adobe Photoshop
Paper/Materials: 80# McCoy Velour
Cover, Gloss UV Coating

Louey/Rubino Design Group

0954
Art Director: Robert Louey
Designers: Robert Louey, Javier
Leguizamo
Client: Louey/Rubino Design Group
Software/Hardware: Quark XPress
Paper/Materials: Fox River Paper

Love Communication

0681
Art Director: Preston Wood
Designer: Craig Lee
Client: Novell Utah Showdown
Software/Hardware: Adobe Photoshop,
Adobe Illustrator, Quark XPress
Paper/Materials: 80lb Cover Lustro

0666
Art Director: Preston Wood
Designer: Preston Wood
Client: Love Communication
Software/Hardware: Adobe Photoshop,

Quark XPress, Adobe Illustrator
Paper/Materials: Pain Can, Confetti,
Lustro Dull

0876
Art Director: Preston Wood
Designer: Craig Lee
Client: Green Space Design
Software/Hardware: Adobe Photoshop,
Quark XPress, Adobe Illustrator
Paper/Materials: French Cordform

m

MA & Associados

0103
Art Director: Mario Aurelio
Designer: Mario Aurelio
Client: MCI
Software/Hardware: Mac, Macromedia
Freehand
Paper/Materials: Couchet

0504
Art Director: Mario Aurelio
Designer: Mario Aurelio
Client: Fuel
Software/Hardware: Mac, Macromedia
Freehand
Paper/Materials: Couchet Mate

0522
Art Director: Mario Aurelio
Designer: Mario Aurelio
Client: Onara
Software/Hardware: Mac, Macromedia
Freehand
Paper/Materials: Couchet

0559
Art Director: Mario Aurelio
Designer: Mario Aurelio
Client: Inovacao
Software/Hardware: Mac, Macromedia
Freehand
Paper/Materials: Couchet Mate

0663
Art Director: Mario Aurelio
Designer: Mario Aurelio
Client: MCI
Software/Hardware: Mac, Macromedia
Freehand
Paper/Materials: Couchet Mate

0651
Art Director: Mario Aurelio
Designer: Mario Aurelio

Client: Fuel
Software/Hardware: Mac, Macromedia
Freehand
Paper/Materials: Ikonofix

0737
Art Director: Mario Aurelio
Designer: Mario Aurelio
Client: Onara
Software/Hardware: Mac, Macromedia
Freehand
Paper/Materials: Star Dream

0820
Art Director: Mario Aurelio
Designer: Mario Aurelio
Client: Fuel
Software/Hardware: Mac, Macromedia
Freehand
Paper/Materials: Star Dream

M-Art

0567
Art Director: Marty Ittner
Designer: Marty Ittner
Client: Rae Rosenthal
Software/Hardware: Quark XPress,
Macromedia Freehand
Paper/Materials: Classic Columns,
Screenprint & Silver Seal

0846
Art Director: Marty Ittner
Designer: Marty Ittner
Client: National Osteoporosis
Foundation
Software/Hardware: Quark XPress,
Macromedia Freehand
Paper/Materials: Strathmore Elements,
Gilclear, Fraser Passport

Maren Bottger

0441
Client: Family of Designer
Software/Hardware: Macromedia
Freehand, Adobe Photoshop, Mac OS
Paper/Materials: Laser Print on Card

0740
Client: Family of Designer
Software/Hardware: Macromedia
Freehand, Mac OS
Paper/Materials: Various Paper & Card,
Round Metal Paperclips

Marlena Sang

0830
Client: Friends
Software/Hardware: Quark XPress
Paper/Materials: Munken Pure 240gm3,
Envelope, Cromatico Zinnober

Martin Lemelman Illustration

0400
Art Director: Martin Lemelman
Client: Martin Lemelman
Software/Hardware: Mac, Adobe
Illustrator

Marty Blake Graphic Design

0452
Art Director: Marty Blake
Designer: Marty Blake
Client: Parmigiano Reggiano, U.S. Office
Software/Hardware: Mac, Adobe
Illustrator, Fotographer
Paper/Materials: Fox River, Sundance,
Confetti

0692
Art Director: Marty Blake
Designer: Marty Blake
Client: Everson Museum of Art
Software/Hardware: Mac, Adobe
Photoshop, Quark XPress
Paper/Materials: Silk- Job Parilux

Matsumoto Incorporated

0074
Art Director: Takaaki Matsumoto
Designer: Takaaki Matsumoto
Client: Matsumoto Incorporated
Software/Hardware: Quark XPress
Paper/Materials: Letterpress, Somerset
White Velvet, 300 gm

0334
Art Director: Takaaki Matsumoto
Designer: Takaaki Matsumoto
Client: Matsumoto Incorporated
Software/Hardware: Quark XPress
Paper/Materials: Offset printing with
Metallic Inks, Neenah Classic Cream
130lb Cover

McCullough Creative Group, Inc.

0216
Designer: McCullough Creative Team
Client: McCullough Creative Group

Software/Hardware: Adobe Photoshop,
Macromedia Freehand, Mac
Paper/Materials: Ribbon, Tinsel,
Ornament Hooks

0248
Designer: Greg Dietzenbach
Client: McCullough Creative Group
Software/Hardware: Macromedia
Freehand, Mac
Paper/Materials: Wire Spiral-Bound

0538
Designer: Erin Germain
Client: Dubuque Bank & Trust
Software/Hardware: Quark/Mac
Paper/Materials: Copper grommet bind-
ing, Wausau Royal Fiber paperstock

0549
Designer: Roger Scholbrock
Client: John Deere Construction &
Forestry Company
Software/Hardware: Adobe Photoshop,
Macromedia Freehand, Mac
Paper/Materials: Wooden Dowel,
Rubber Band

McGINTY

0276
Art Director: Matt Rue
Designers: Matt Rue, Kyle Russell
Software/Hardware: Adobe Photoshop

Megan Cooney

0061
Client: Megan Cooney

0578
Client: Megan Cooney

Megan Webber Design

0141
Designers: Megan Webber, Wendy
Carnegie
Client: Megan Webber
Software/Hardware: Adobe Illustrator
Paper/Materials: Verigood Blotting,
Letterpress Printing

0185
Designer: Megan Webber
Client: Megan Webber Design
Software/Hardware: Adobe Illustrator
Paper/Materials: 1-Color Silk-Screen on
Carnival White 65#C

0378

Designers: Megan Webber, Wendy Carnegie,
Julie Savakis
Client: Megan Webber
Software/Hardware: Adobe Illustrator
Paper/Materials: Vertigos Blotting,
2-Color Letterpress

Metzler & Associes

0153

Art Director: M. A. Herrmann
Designer: A. Pavion
Client: Metzler & Associes
Software/Hardware: Adobe Illustrator,
Macromedia Flash MX

0271

Art Director: M.A. Herrmann
Designer: A. Martirene
Client: Metzler & Associes
Software/Hardware: Adobe Illustrator,
Mac

Michael Courtney Design

0511

Art Director: Michael Courtney
Designer: Michael Courtney
Client: Christine O'Leary
Software/Hardware: Macromedia
Freehand

0547

Art Director: Michael Courtney
Designers: Heidi Fanour, Michael
Courtney, Margaret Longi
Client: Bellevue Arts Commission
Software/Hardware: Macromedia
Freehand, Adobe Photoshop

0570

Art Director: Michael Courtney
Designers: Micahel Courtney, Debra
Burgess
Client: Tops Art Fest
Software/Hardware: Macromedia
Freehand, Adobe Photoshop
Paper/Materials: Cut Paper, Pastel,
Marker

0928

Art Director: Michael Courtney
Designers: Michael Courtney, Karen
Cramer,
Heidi Favour, Margaret Long, Jennifer
Comer, Lauren DiRusso
Client: Michael Courtney Design

Software/Hardware: Macromedia
Freehand, Adobe Photoshop
Paper/Materials: Embossed Paper,
Copper Tag (Etched), 4/C Offset on
Uncoated Stock, Vellum

Michael Osborne Design

0024

Art Director: Michael Osborne
Client: Michael Osborne Design
Software/Hardware: Adobe Illustrator,
Mac
Paper/Materials: Summerset

0117

Art Director: Michael Osborne
Designer: Michelle Regenbogen
Client: Michael Osborne Design
Software/Hardware: Adobe Illustrator,
Mac
Paper/Materials: Summerset

0269

Art Director: Michael Osborne
Designers: Paul Kagiwada/Michelle
Regen Bogen
Client: Michael Osborne Design
Software/Hardware: Adobe Illustrator,
Mac
Paper/Materials: Strathmore

0358

Art Director: Michael Osborne
Client: Michael Osborne Design
Software/Hardware: Adobe Illustrator,
Mac
Paper/Materials: Cranes

0934

Art Director: Michael Osborne
Designer: Michelle Regenbogen
Client: Fox River Paper
Software/Hardware: Adobe Illustrator,
Mac
Paper/Materials: Starwhite

Mike Quon/Designation

0871

Art Director: Mike Quon
Designer: Mike Quon
Client: Mike Quon/Tulsa ADC
Software/Hardware: Adobe Illustrator,
Mac
Paper/Materials: Cover Stock

Milk Row Studio/Press

0018

Art Director: Keith D. Cross
Designer: Keith D. Cross
Client: (self-promotional greeting)
Paper/Materials: Metal, Ink, Paper,
Press, Hand Set Type & Ornamenes
Printed Letterpress on Neenah Solar
White 110 lb. Cover

0677

Art Director: Keith D. Cross
Designer: Keith D. Cross
Client: The Letterpress Guild of New
England
Paper/Materials: Metal, Ink, Paper,
Press, Handset Type, Ornaments
Printed Letterpress on Neenah, Classic
Crest, Ember Blue 80lb. Cover

0640

Art Director: Keith D. Cross
Designer: Keith D. Cross
Client: Peter Pinch & Catherine Yu
Software/Hardware: Metal, Ink, Paper,
Press
Paper/Materials: Linocut Illustrations,
Handset Type, Neenah Saw Grass,
80lb. Cover

0777

Art Director: Keith D. Cross
Designer: Keith D. Cross
Client: Allen Hiltz & Erin McGee
Software/Hardware: Adobe Photoshop
6.0, Macromedia Freehand 9.0
Paper/Materials: Metal, Ink, Paper,
Press, Handset Type & Illustration
Printed from Plate,
Gilbert Voice Slate & Chalk

Mindwalk Design Group, Inc.

0238

Art Director: Michael Huggins
Client: Mindwalk Design Group
Software/Hardware: Adobe Illustrator,
Quark Express, Mac

Miro Design

0027, 0028, 0094, 0159, 0160, 0161,
0162, 0270
Designer: Judy Glenzer
Client: Aardvark Letterpress/Syndicate
Design
Software/Hardware: Adobe Illustrator
Paper/Materials: Lana Watercolor Paper

Mirage Design

0317, 0349

Art Director: Mark LaPointe
Designer: Lynette Allaire
Client: Mirage Design
Software/Hardware: Macromedia
Freehand, Mac

0716

Art Director: Mark LaPointe
Designer: Lynette Allaire
Client: Boston Municipal Research
Bureau
Software/Hardware: Macromedia
Freehand, Mac

0837

Art Director: Mark LaPointe
Designer: Lynette Allaire
Client: Massachusetts High Technology
Council
Software/Hardware: Macromedia
Freehand, Mac

Mirko Ilić Corp

0454

Art Director: Mirko Ilić
Designers: Mirko Ilić, Heath Hingardner
Client: Levy Creative

0609

Art Director: Mirko Ilić
Designers: Mirko Ilić, Heath Hingardner
Client: Auschwitz Jewish Center

0908

Art Director: Mirko Ilić
Designer: Mirko Ilić
Client: K-Space

Misha Design Studio

0018

Art Director: Misha Lenn
Designer: Misha Lenn
Client: City of Boston
Software/Hardware: Watercolor

0073

Art Director: Misha Lenn
Designer: Misha Lenn
Client: Boston Symphony Orchestra
Paper/Materials: Watercolor

0116

Art Director: Misha Lenn
Designer: Misha Lenn
Client: Filene's Basement
Paper/Materials: Naturoles

M. J. Bronstein

0275

Art Director: M. J. Bronstein
Designer: M. J. Bronstein
Client: M. J. Bronstein
Software/Hardware: Adobe Photoshop,
Mac OS
Paper/Materials: Ultra Premium Brilliant
White Card Stock with Aqueous Coating

Momentum Press and Design

0906

Art Director: Jill Vartenigian
Designer: Jill Vartenigian
Client: Kathleen Kenneally Acupuncture
Paper/Materials: Wood Type, Lead
Type, Rives BFK, Letterpress Printed
On a 10X15 C & P

Muse Inspired

0036, 0037, 0038, 0355, 0357

Art Director: Victoria Kens
Designer: Victoria Kens
Client: Muse Inspired

Muzak Marketing

0829

Art Director: Bob Finigan
Designer: David Eller
Client: Muzak
Software/Hardware: Macromedia
Freehand 10, Mac
Paper Materials: Self-Sealing Poly
Envelope, Fasson Fastrack Pressure
Sensitive Label,
60 lb. Recycled Lynx Opaque Smooth
Finish

0892

Art Director: Bob Finigan
Designer: David Eller
Client: Muzak
Software/Hardware: Macromedia
Freehand 10, Mac
Paper/Materials: Inserts – Mohawk
Options TrueWhite, 96 Smooth 130 dic;
Envelope – Mohawk Options TrueWhite,
96 Vellum 130 dic

0885

Art Director: Bob Finigan
Designer: David Eller
Client: Muzak and Karim Rashid, Inc.
Software/Hardware: Macromedia
Freehand 10, Mac

Paper/Materials: 60 lb. Recycled Lynx
Opaque Smooth Finish

0994

Designer: David Eller
Client: Muzak & Karim Rashid, Inc.
Software/Hardware: Macromedia
Freehand 10, Mac
Paper/Materials: Laminated Film Pouch,
Heat-Sealed, 100lb Starwhite Mohawk,
Superfine Cover, Ultra White

n

Nassar Design

0078

Art Director: Nelida Nassar
Designers: Margarita Encomienda,
Nelida Nassar
Client: Nassar Design
Software/Hardware: Quark XPress
Paper/Materials: Gross Grain Ribbon &
#100 Text Onancock Dulcet Smooth

0114

Art Director: Nelida Nassar
Designers: Margarita Encomienda,
Nelida Nassar
Client: Nassar Design
Software/Hardware: Quark XPress,
Adobe Photoshop
Paper/Materials: #30 Text Chartham
Translucents Platinum, #27 Chromatic
Flue Pink
Envelope #27 Chromatic Mango

0211

Art Director: Nelida Nassar
Designers: Margarita Encomienda,
Nelida Nassar
Client: Hybrid
Software/Hardware: Quark XPress,
Adobe Illustrator
Paper/Materials:12pt One-Side Cover
Kromekote Glass

0241

Art Director: Nelida Nassar
Designers: Margarita Encomienda,
Nelida Nassar
Client: Weidlinger Associates, Inc.
Software/Hardware: Quark XPress,
Adobe Photoshop, Adobe Illustrator
Paper/Materials: #92 Cover Arjo Wiggins
Keaykolour Metallics Anodized
Envelope #20 Chartham Translucents
Ocean Blue

0239

Art Director: Nelida Nassar
Designers: Margarita Encomienda,
Nelida Nassar
Client: Sea-Dar Enterprises
Software/Hardware: Quark XPress,
Adobe Illustrator
Paper/Materials: #100 cover Mohawk
Superfine Ultrawhite Smooth

0290

Art Director: Nelida Nassar
Designers: Margarita Encomienda,
Nelida Nassar
Client: Nassar Design
Software/Hardware: Quark XPress
Paper/Materials: Mylar Cracked Ice
Burgundy

0405

Art Director: Nelida Nassar
Designers: Margarita Encomienda,
Nelida Nassar
Client: The Stubbins Associates, Inc.
Software/Hardware: Quark XPress,
Adobe Illustrator
Paper/Materials: #53 Cover Arjo Wiggins
Curious Translucent Gold Iridescent

0425

Art Director: Nelida Nassar
Designers: Margarita Encomienda,
Nelida Nassar
Client: Weidlinger Associates, Inc.
Software/Hardware: Quark XPress,
Adobe Photoshop
Paper/Materials: #100 Cover Mohawk
Superfine White plus Matching
Envelopes

0466

Art Director: Nelida Design
Designers: Margarita Encomienda,
Nelida Nassar
Client: The Stubbins Associates, Inc.
Software/Hardware: Quark XPress,
Adobe Illustrator
Paper/Materials: #80 Cover Sappi
Strobe Silk

0653

Art Director: Nelida Nassar
Designers: Margarita Encomienda,
Nelida Nassar
Client: Artisans du Liban et d'Orient
Software/Hardware: Quark XPress,
Adobe Illustrator
Paper/Materials: #92.5 Cover Zanders
Ikono Dull Satin

0689

Art Director: Nelida Nassar
Designers: Margarita Encomienda,
Nelida Nassar
Client: Harvard Design School
Software/Hardware: Quark XPress,
Adobe Illustrator
Paper/Materials: #100 Cover Sappi
Vintage Gloss

0827

Art Director: Nelida Nassar
Designers: Margarita Encomienda,
Nelida Nassar
Client: Harvard Design School
Software/Hardware: Quark XPress,
Adobe Photoshop
Paper/Materials: #100 Mohawk
Superfine Ultrawhite Smooth Double-
Thick

0880

Art Director: Nelida Nassar
Designers: Margarita Encomienda,
Nelida Nassar
Client: Weidlinger Associates, Inc.
Software/Hardware: Quark XPress,
Adobe Photoshop, Adobe Illustrator
Paper/Materials: #92 Cover Arjo Wiggins
Keaykolour Metallics Galvanised

0915

Art Director: Nelida Nassar
Designers: Margarita Encomienda,
Nelida Nassar
Client: Jacques Liger-Belair
Software/Hardware: Quark XPress,
Adobe Illustrator
Paper/Materials: #92.5 Cover Zanders
Ikono Matt

0944

Art Director: Nelida Nassar
Designers: Margarita Encomienda,
Nelida Nassar
Client: Leers Weizapfel Architects
Associates, Inc.
Software/Hardware: Quark Xpress,
Adobe Illustrator
Paper/Materials: #80 Cover Sappi
Vintage Velvet

0997

Art Director: Nelida Nassar
Designers: Margarita Encomienda,
Nelida Nassar
Client: The Stubbins Associates, Inc.
Software/Hardware: Quark XPress,
Adobe Photoshop

Paper/Materials: #80 Cover Sappi Strobe Silk

New Idea Design

0552
Designer: Ron Boldt
Client: Regional West Medical Center
Software/Hardware: Macromedia
Freehand 7.0, Mac

Nexus

0362
Art Director: Arvi Raquel-Santos
Designer: Avvi Raquel-Santos
Client: Self-Promotion Christmas Card
Software/Hardware: Adobe Illustrator, Mac
Paper/Materials: Colored Pencil (Hand Colored)

Nickelodeon Creative Resources

0507
Art Director: Theresa Fitzgerald
Designer: Erin Blankley
Client: Klasky-Csupo
Software/Hardware: Adobe Illustrator
Paper/Materials: Semigloss Cardstock, Z Metallic Inks, Star Confetti

Nielinger & Rohsiepe

0209
Photographer: Christian Nielinger
Designer: Herbert Rohsiepe
Client: Christian Nielinger & Herbert Rohsiepe
Software/Hardware: Macromedia Freehand, Mac
Paper/Materials: Arjo Wiggins Impressions

9SpotMonk Design Co.

0465
Art Director: Vivian Leung
Designer: Vivian Leung
Client: Jill & Paul Roebinson
Software/Hardware: Macromedia Freehand MX
Paper/Materials: Arches Paper, Cromatica Envelopes Printed via Letterpress

0484
Art Director: Vivian Leung
Designer: Vivian Leung

Client: Jill & Paul Roebinson
Software/Hardware: Macromedia Freehand MX
Paper/Materials: Arches Paper, Cromatica Envelopes

0583
Art Director: Vivian Leung
Designer: Vivian Leung
Client: Marjorie Slatin & Diego Vasquez
Software/Hardware: Mac, Macromedia Freehand MX
Paper/Materials: Pescia Paper, Custom Envelope, Printed Via Letterpress

0585
Art Director: Vivian Leung
Designer: Vivian Leung
Client: Vivian Leung & Erik Naranjo
Software/Hardware: Mac, Macromedia Freehand MX
Paper/Materials: Somerset Cards, Arturo Envelopes, Printed via Letterpress

0561
Art Director: Vivian Leung
Designer: Vivian Leung
Client: Margrethe Jacobson & Collin McDermott
Software/Hardware: Mac, Macromedia Freehand MX
Paper/Materials: Somerset paper, Arturo Envelopes, Printed via Letterpress

0630
Art Director: Vivian Leung
Designer: Vivian Leung
Client: Catalina Grimaldi & Stephano DiAlessandro
Software/Hardware: Mac, Macromedia Freehand MX
Paper/Materials: Somerset Paper, Arturo Envelope, Printed via Letterpress

Noon

0448
Art Director: Cinthia Wen
Designer: Cinthia Wen
Client: Greg Shove
Software/Hardware: Adobe Photoshop, Adobe Illustrator, Mac

0898
Art Director: Cinthia Wen
Designer: Claudia Fung
Software/Hardware: Adobe Illustrator, Mac

Paper/Materials: Starwhite Vicksburg, Fresh Rosemary

0938
Art Director: Cinthia Wen
Designer: Cinthia Wen
Software/Hardware: Adobe Illustrator, Mac
Paper/Materials: Handmade Paper, Gmund Envelopes (GER)

O

OrangeSeed Design

0648
Art Director: Damien Wolf
Designers: Damien Wolf, Rebecca Miles
Client: Andersen Corporation
Software/Hardware: Adobe Photoshop, Quark XPress, Mac G4
Paper/Materials: Curious Papers, Anodized & Ice Gold 92lb Cover, Anodized A7 Envelopes

0972
Art Director: Damien Wolf
Designers: Damien Wolf, Phil Hoch
Client: OrangeSeed Design
Software/Hardware: Adobe Illustrator, Adobe Photoshop, Quark XPress, Mac G4
Paper/Materials: Wood Orange Crate & Anchor Paper-Proterra Straw 70lb Text

p

Palm Press

0012
Art Director: Theresa McCormac
Client: Retail Sales

Palo Alto Junior Museum & Zoo

0158
Designer: Efrat Rafaeli
Client: Palo Alto Junior Museum & Zoo
Software/Hardware: Adobe Illustrator
Paper/Materials: Carolina CISO

0765
Designer: Efrat Rafaeli
Client: Palo Alto Junior Museum & Zoo
Software/Hardware: Adobe Illustrator
Paper/Materials: Cougar

0799
Designer: Efrat Rafaeli
Client: Palo Alto Junior Museum & Zoo
Software/Hardware: Adobe Illustrator
Paper/Materials: Card Stock

Pangaro Beer

0007
Art Directors: Natalie Pangaro, Shannon Beer
Designers: Natalie Pangaro, Shannon Beer
Client: Pangaro Beer
Software/Hardware: Quark XPress 4.0
Paper/Materials: Strathmore-Ultimate White 80# Cover

0341
Art Directors: Natalie Pangard, Shannon Beer
Designers: David Salafia, Joanna DeFazio
Client: Pangard Beer
Software/Hardware: Quark XPress
Paper/Materials: Strathmore

0558
Art Directors: Natalie Pangard, Shannon Beer
Designer: David Salafia
Client: Harvard Medical School
Software/Hardware: Quark XPress 4.0
Paper/Materials: Gilbert Realm

0604
Art Directors: Natalie Pangard, Shannon Beer
Designer: David Salafia
Client: Harvard Medical School
Software/Hardware: Quark XPress 4.0
Paper/Materials: Gilbert Realm, Natural

0652
Art Directors: Natalie Pangard, Shannon Beer
Designer: David Salafia
Client: Mellon
Software/Hardware: Quark XPress 4.0

0754
Art Directors: Natalie Pangard, Shannon Beer
Designers: David Salafia, Joanna DeFazio
Client: The Art Institute of Boston
Software/Hardware: Quark XPress 4.0
Paper/Materials: Scheufelen, Phoendstarr 80# Cover Dull

Paper Lantern Press

0050
Art Director: Michelle Farinella
Designer: Michelle Farinella
Client: Paper Lantern Press
Software/Hardware: Mac, Quark XPress, Adobe Photoshop
Paper/Materials: Gilbert Realm

0150
Art Director: Michelle Farinella
Designers: Michelle Farinella, Judith Wolf
Client: Paper Lantern Press
Software/Hardware: Quark XPress, Mac, Adobe Photoshop
Paper/Materials: Gilbert Realm

0152
Art Director: Michelle Farinella
Designers: Michelle Farinella, Judith Wolf
Client: Paper Lantern Press
Software/Hardware: Mac, Quark XPress, Adobe Photoshop
Paper/Materials: Vintage Velvet

Partners in Print

0764
Art Director: Ariel Janzen
Designer: Ariel Janzen
Client: Laurel Crockett, Drew Rector
Software/Hardware: Adobe Illustrator
Paper/Materials: Vellum, Handmade Papers, Original Calligraphy

Paul Shaw Letter Design

0389
Designer: Paul Shaw
Client: Paul Shaw Letter Design & Peter Kruty Editions

Peggy Pelletier

0035, 0090, 0091, 0359, 0360
Paper/Materials: Handmade Swatchbook Scraps, Old Paper Promotions

Pernsteiner Creative Group, Inc.

0684
Art Director: Todd Pernsteiner
Designer: Andy Hauck
Client: County Concrete Corporation
Software/Hardware: Adobe Photoshop, Quark XPress, Mac
Paper/Materials: 125# Manilla Tag, 100# Mounte Matte Text

Peter Kruty Editions

0409
Designer: Alexander Ku
Client: Alexander Ku & Jane Yemzas Ku

0806
Designer: Sayre Gaydos
Client: Kristin Newman Designs

0833
Designer: Sayre Gaydos

plus design, inc.

0062
Art Director: Anita Meyer
Designer: Anita Meyer
Software/Hardware: Quark XPress, by Hand
Paper/Materials: Curious Paper Bronze Ore, Cover 92 lb, Tissue Paper, Ribbon, Silver Thread

0417
Art Directors: Anita Meyer, Karin Fickett, Dina Zaccagnini, Matthew Monk
Designers: Anita Meyer, Karin Fickett, Dina Zaccagnini, Matthew Monk, Jan Baker
Client: Plus Design, Inc.
Paper/Materials: Cloth, Silkscreener

0510
Art Director: Anita Meyer
Designers: Anita Meyer, Vivian Law
Client: Princeton University Art Museum
Software/Hardware: Quark XPress, Mac

0568
Art Director: Anita Meyer
Designer: Anita Meyer
Client: The Cloud Foundation
Software/Hardware: Quark XPress, Mac

0496
Art Director: Anita Meyer
Designers: Anita Meyer, Jan Baker
Client: plus design inc.
Software/Hardware: Letterpress
Paper/Materials: Handmade Paper-Made from Old Sheets, Cloth, Flowers, Hair & Books

0949
Art Directors: Anita Meyer, Karin Fickett

Designers: Anita Meyer, Vivian Law, Karin Fickett, Kristin Hughes
Client: Plus Design, Inc.
Software/Hardware: Quark Xpress, Mac
Paper/Materials: Recycled press sheets, static shielding bag, carpentry pencils
Title: New Year's Gift

Popcorn Initiative

0070
Art Directors: Chris Jones, Roger Wood
Designers: Chris Jones, Roger Wood
Client: Popcorn Initiative
Software/Hardware: Mac G4-500 Megahertz, 5" X 8" Kelsey, Excelsior LetterPress
Paper/Materials: French Paper, Frostone 140 lb. Cover, Glacier & Lots of Wire

0762
Art Directors: Chris Jones, Roger Wood
Designers: Chris Jones, Roger Wood
Client: Popcorn Initiative
Software/Hardware: Mac G4-500 Megahertz
Paper/Materials: Table Saw, Via Paper, White 100lb Text, Burlap & Grommets

Porto & Martinez Design Studio

0432
Art Directors: Bruno Porto, Marcelo Martinez
Designer: Bruno Porto
Client: Madina Artes Graficas
Software/Hardware: Quark XPress, Mac, Adobe Photoshop
Paper/Materials: 4-Color Die-Cut Popup

0828
Art Directors: Marcelo Martinez, Bruno Porto
Designer/Illustrator: Marcelo Martinez
Client: Marcelo Martinez, Renata Arlota
Software/Hardware: Quark XPress, Macromedia Freehand, Adobe Photoshop, Mac
Paper/Materials: Color Print on Elements, Soft White Dots 216g

Prank

0703
Client: Art Institute of Boston Class of '03

Paper/Materials: Silkscreen, Hanes Size 4 Boys

Pure Imagination Studios

0801
Art Director: Josh Williams
Designer: Josh Williams
Client: Rachel & Josh Williams
Software/Hardware: Penlink, Macromedia Freehand, Mac OS 10
Paper/Materials: Strathmore Writing Cover, Neenah Uv ultra II

r

R2 design

0693
Art Directors: Liza Defossez Ramalho, Artur Rebelo
Designers: Lize Defossez Ramalho & Artur Rebelo
Client: Marta & Gil
Software/Hardware: Macromedia Freehand 9.0
Paper/Materials: Recycled Cardboard, Bright Paper

0864
Art Directors: Liza Defossez Ramalho, Artur Rebelo
Designers: Liza Defossez Ramalho, Artur Rebelo
Client: Cassiopeia
Software/Hardware: Macromedia Freehand 9.0
Paper/Materials: Recycled Cardboard

Range

0499
Art Director: Steve Richard
Designer: Amy Becker-Jones
Client: Canton High School-Class of 1993 Reunion
Software/Hardware: Quark XPress, Adobe Photoshop, Mac
Paper/Materials: French Paper, Starch White, 120 lb Cover, Hand Silk Screened

0564
Art Director: Steve Richard
Client: Juvenile Diabetes Research Foundation-NH

Software/Hardware: Quark XPress, Adobe Photoshop
Paper/Materials: Domtar Feltweave

Red Design

0127
Art Director: Red Design
Designer: Red Design
Client: Red Design
Software/Hardware: Macromedia Freehand, Mac
Paper/Materials: Card

0410
Art Director: Red Design
Designer: Red Design
Client: Ourselves
Software/Hardware: Macromedia Freehand
Paper/Materials: Wood

Red Alert Design

0920
Art Directors: Jon Wainwright, Matt Sanerman
Designers: Jon Wainwright, Matt Sanderman
Client: Red Alert Design
Software/Hardware: Adobe Illustrator, Mac
Paper/Materials: Inflatable Plastic Bag, Screen Print

Refinery Design Company

0105, 0348, 0787
Art Director: Mike Schmalz
Designer: Julie Schmalz
Client: DHCU
Software/Hardware: Mac, Macromedia Freehand

0576
Art Director: Mike Schmalz
Designer: Julie Schmalz
Client: Joe & Trisha Hearn
Software/Hardware: Mac, Macromedia Freehand

0825
Art Director: Mike Schmalz
Designer: Julie Schmalz
Client: Rick & Kim Dehn
Software/Hardware: Mac, Micromedia Freehand

0636
Art Director: Mike Schmalz

Designer: Mike Schmalz
Client: Mike & Julie Schmalz
Software/Hardware: Mac, Macromedia Freehand

re.salzman designs

0840
Art Directors: Rick Salzman, Ida Cheinman
Designers: Rick Salzman, Ida Cheinman
Client: Adler Display
Software/Hardware: Mac, Adobe Illustrator 10
Paper/Materials: 120lb Cover, Dull Productolith

Rick Johnson & Company

0109
Art Director: Mark Chamblain
Designer: Tim McGrath
Client: United Blood Services
Software/Hardware: Quark XPress, Mac
Paper/Materials: Candy Box, White Candy Cane

0627
Designer: Tim McGrath
Client: Los Alamos National Bank
Software/Hardware: Quark XPress, Adobe Illustrator
Paper/Materials: Classic Crest

0849
Designer: Tim McGrath
Client: Los Alamos National Bank
Software/Hardware: Quark XPress, Adobe Illustrator

0862
Designer: Tim McGrath
Client: N.M. Advertising Federation
Software/Hardware: Quark XPress, Adobe Illustrator

Rick Rawlins/Work

0030
Art Director: Rick Rawlins
Designer: Rick Rawlins
Client: Eleven
Software/Hardware: Quark XPress, Mac
Paper/Materials: Slate

0429
Art Director: Rick Rawlins
Designer: Rick Rawlins
Client: Nathan & Bridget Rawlins
Software/Hardware: Quark XPress, Mac

Paper/Materials: Mallard Feather & Metal tin

0469
Art Director: Rick Rawlins
Designer: Rick Rawlins
Client: The Cambridge Arts Council
Software/Hardware: Quark XPress, Mac
Paper/Materials: Chipboard, Glow-in-the-Dark Ink

0497
Art Director: Rick Rawlins
Designer: Rick Rawlins
Client: Daryl Otte
Software/Hardware: Mac, Quark XPress
Paper/Materials: Rives BFK, Apron, Glassine, Kraft

0587
Art Director: Rick Rawlins
Designer: Rick Rawlins
Client: Eleven
Software/Hardware: Quark XPress, Mac
Paper/Materials: Bandanas, Thermochromatic Bookmarks

0596
Art Director: Rick Rawlins
Designer: Rick Rawlins
Client: Cambridge Peace Commission
Software/Hardware: Quark XPress, Mac
Paper/Materials: Black board, Candle, and Newsprint

0626
Art Director: Rick Rawlins
Designer: Rick Rawlins
Client: Art Institute of Boston
Software/Hardware: Quark XPress, Mac

0682
Art Director: Rick Rawlins
Designer: Rick Rawlins
Client: Art Institute of Boston
Software/Hardware: Quark XPress, Mac
Paper/Materials: Van Gelder, Cotton Linter

0800
Art Director: Rick Rawlins
Designer: Rick Rawlins
Client: Wellesley College
Software/Hardware: Quark XPress, Mac
Paper/Materials: Pharmaceutical Packaging, Glassine

0724
Art Director: Rick Rawlins
Designers: Rick Rawlins, Manuel Ortega

Client: Letterpress Guild of New England
Software/Hardware: Quark XPress, Mac
Paper/Materials: Newsprint, Kraft

0872
Art Director: Rick Rawlins
Designer: Rick Rawlins
Client: The Cambridge Arts Council
Software/Hardware: Quark XPress, Mac

0779, 0797
Art Director: Rick Rawlins
Designer: Rick Rawlins
Client: Isabella Stewart Gardner Museum
Software/Hardware: Quark XPress, Mac

0922
Art Director: Rick Rawlins
Designer: Rick Rawlins
Client: Carl Tremblay
Software/Hardware: Quark XPress, Letter Press
Paper/Materials: Kraft

0951
Art Director: Rick Rawlins
Designer: Rick Rawlins
Client: Genesis
Software/Hardware: Quark XPress, Mac
Paper/Materials: Template Plastic

Rickabaugh Graphics

0230
Art Director: Eric Rickabaugh
Designer: Eric Rickabaugh
Client: Rickabaugh Graphics
Software/Hardware: Macromedia Freehand, Mac

Riordon Design

0075
Art Director: Dan Wheaton
Designers: Shirley Riordon, Amy Montgomery
Client: In-Sync
Software/Hardware: Mac, Quark XPress, Adobe Illustrator
Paper/Materials: Crushed Leaf & Chartham Translucents for A-7 Envelope

0174
Art Director: Dan Wheaton
Designer: Amy Montgomery
Client: Riordon Design

Software/Hardware: Mac, Quark XPress, Adobe Illustrator
Paper/Materials: Euroart

0201
Art Director: Dan Wheaton
Designer: Tim Warnock
Client: Riordon Design
Software/Hardware: Mac, Adobe Photoshop, Quark XPress
Paper/Materials: Euroart, A-7 Charthem Translucents, Envelope

0253
Art Director: Dan Wheaton
Designer: Tim Warnock
Client: X-Eye
Software/Hardware: Mac, Adobe Photoshop, Quark XPress
Paper/Materials: Euroart

0268
Art Director: Dan Wheaton
Designers: Amy Montgomery, Sharon Pece
Client: Riordon Design
Software/Hardware: Quark XPress, Adobe Illustrator, Adobe Photoshop
Paper/Materials: Neenah Environment

0858
Art Director: Dan Wheaton
Designer: Sharon Pece
Client: M for Men
Software/Hardware: Quark XPress
Paper/Materials: Curious Metallics, A-7 Envelope-Chartham Translucents

0774
Art Director: Dan Wheaton
Designers: Cori Hellard, Tim Warnock, Shirley Riordon, Dan Wheaton
Client: Scotia Capital
Software/Hardware: Mac, Quark XPress, Adobe Illustrator, Adobe Photoshop
Paper/Materials: Various Papers & Fabrics

Rob Kimmell

0838
Client: Rob Kimmell & Kristin Jensen

Robilant & Associates

0957
Art Director: Maurizio DiRobilant
Designer: Maurizio DiRobilant
Client: Self-Promotion

Paper/Materials: Aluminium Can with Olive Oil

Rome & Gold Creative

0113
Art Director: Robert E. Goldie
Designer: Lorenzo Romero
Client: Calvary of Albuquerque
Software/Hardware: Adobe Illustrator, Adobe Photoshop

0742
Art Director: Robert E. Goldie
Designers: Lorenzo Romero, Zeke Sikelianos
Client: Tri Progress Productions
Software/Hardware: Adobe Photoshop, Adobe Illustrator
Paper/Materials: Tickets & Envelopes, French Paper Co. Durotone Butcher Black

Rosalia Nocerino

0528
Designer: Rosalia Nocerino
Client: Rosalia Nocerino, Frances Bonanni
Software/Hardware: Quark XPress, Mac
Paper/Materials: Cromatica (aqua), Strathmore Elements

0560
Designer: Rosalia Nocerino
Client: Katie Couric
Software/Hardware: Quark XPress, Adobe Illustrator, Mac
Paper/Materials: Cromatica (Yellow)

0770
Designer: Rosalia Nocerino
Client: Self
Software/Hardware: Quark XPress, Mac
Paper/Materials: Wausau Celebrations in Ivory & Gillmore Oxford Vellum

Roundel

0274
Art Director: John Bateson
Designer: Paul Ingle
Client: Doric Signs
Software/Hardware: Mac, Quark Xpress

0463
Art Director: John Bateson
Designer: Paul Ingle
Client: Chantel Desforges
Software/Hardware: Mac, Quark XPress

0615
Art Director: John Bateson
Designer: Paul Ingle
Client: Design Business Association
Software/Hardware: Mac, Quark XPress
Paper/Materials: Chromolux Magic Lips 250gsm

Roycroft Design

0605
Art Director: Jennifer Roycroft
Designer: Jennifer Roycroft
Client: Mohawk Paper Mills
Software/Hardware: Quark XPress, Mac
Paper/Materials: Mohawk Superior

Rule29

0054
Art Directors: Justin Ahrens, Jim Boborci
Designers: Justin Ahrens, Jim Boborci
Client: Rule 29
Software/Hardware: Quark XPress, Mac
Paper/Materials: Pegasus, Synergy

0431
Art Director: Justin Ahrens
Designer: Justin Ahrens
Software/Hardware: Quark XPress, Mac
Paper/Materials: Classic Columns, Sappi McCoy

0455
Art Directors: Justin Ahrens, Jim Boborci
Designers: Justin Ahrens, Jim Boborci
Client: Rule 29
Software/Hardware: Quark XPress, Mac
Paper/Materials: Classic Crest

0524
Art Directors: Justin Ahrens, Jim Boborci
Designers: Justin Ahrens, Jim Boborci
Client: AIGA Chicago
Software/Hardware: Quark XPress, Mac
Paper/Materials: McCoy Uncoated

0720
Art Director: Justin Ahrens
Designer: Jessie Bultema
Client: Lighthouse Marketing
Software/Hardware: Quark XPress, Mac

0737
Art Directors: Jon McGrath, Jessie Bultema

Designers: Jon McGrath, Jessie Bultema
Software/Hardware: Quark XPress, Mac
Paper/Materials: Pegasus

0589
Art Director: Justin Ahrens
Designers: Justin Ahrens, Jon McGrath
Client: Lighthouse Marketing
Software/Hardware: Quark XPress, Mac

0955
Art Directors: Justin Ahrens, Jim Boborci
Designers: Justin Ahrens, Jim Boborci
Client: Rule 29
Software/Hardware: Quark XPress, Mac
Paper/Materials: Pegasus, Synergy

0999
Art Directors: Justin Ahrens, Jim Boborci
Designers: Justin Ahrens, Jim Boborci
Client: Ascentives
Software/Hardware: Quark XPress, Mac
Paper/Materials: Classic Crest

Russell Design

0603
Art Director: Tina Winey
Designer: Laura Ploszaj
Client: City Harvest
Software/Hardware: Adobe Illustrator, Quark XPress
Paper/Materials: Mohawk Superfine

0651
Designer: Dana Snider
Client: Amanda Allen
Software/Hardware: Quark XPress, Adobe Illustrator, Mac

0637
Art Director: Tina Winey
Designer: Laura Ploszaj
Client: City Harvest
Software/Hardware: Quark XPress
Paper/Materials: Envelope-Evanescent, Invitation-Superfine

0808
Designer: Dana Snider
Client: Stephanie Obando
Software/Hardware: Quark XPress, Adobe Illustrator, Mac

0891
Art Director: Tony Russell
Designer: Julie Beard

Client: Russell Design
Software/Hardware: Quark Xpress

0956
Art Director: Tony Russell
Designer: Julie Beard
Client: Nasdaq
Software/Hardware: Quark Xpress

Ruth Hulmerind

0948
Art Director: Ruth Hulmerind
Designer: Juri Loun
Client: Ruth Hulmerind
Software/Hardware: Macromedia Flash 9.0
Paper/Materials: Countryside Mishal

0963
Art Director: Ruth Hulmerind
Designer: Juri Loun
Client: Modo Paper
Software/Hardware: Macromedia Flash 9.0
Paper/Materials: Retreeve Earthtints, Invercote

0979
Art Director: Ruth Hulmerind
Designer: Juri Kass
Client: Modo Paper
Software/Hardware: Macromedia Freehand .0
Paper/Materials: Invercote

0982
Art Director: Ruth Hulmerind
Designer: Juri Loun
Client: MAP Eesti
Software/Hardware: Macromedia Freehand 9.0
Paper/Materials: Evanescent, Invercote, Creato

S

Sagmeister, Inc

0590
Art Director: Stefan Sagmeister
Designer: Hjalti Karlsson
Client: Sagmeister, Inc
Software/Hardware: Adobe Illustrator, Mac
Paper/Materials: Fart Cushion

0655
Art Director: Stefan Sagmeister

Designer: Matthias Arnstberger
Client: Sagmeister
Software/Hardware: Adobe Photoshop, Mac
Paper/Materials: 300 gsm Board

Samata Mason

0878
Art Director: Pat Samata
Designer: Lynne Nagel
Client: Fine Arts Engraving
Software/Hardware: Quark XPress, Adobe Photoshop, Mac
Paper/Materials: Classic Crest 100#, Cover & Text Avalanche White Smooth

Sayles Graphic Design

0106
Art Director: John Sayles
Designers: John Sayles, Som Inthalangsy
Client: Ahmanson Family
Software/Hardware: Adobe Illustrator
Paper/Materials: Cougar Natural 100# Cover

0527
Art Director: John Sayles
Designers: John Sayles, Som Inthalangsy
Client: American Institute of Architects
Software/Hardware: Adobe Illustrator, Quark XPress
Paper/Materials: Mohawk Navajo 80# Cover, Text

0586
Art Director: John Sayles
Designers: John Sayles, Som Inthalangsy
Client: City of Ankeny, Iowa
Software/Hardware: Adobe Illustrator, Quark XPress
Paper/Materials: Cougar 803 Cover Screenprinted on Corrugated Box

0671
Art Director: John Sayles
Designers: John Sayles, Som Inthalangsy
Client: Hewitt Associates
Software/Hardware: Adobe Illustrator
Paper/Materials: Luna Matte 80# Cover

0810
Art Director: John Sayles
Designers: John Sayles, Som

Inthalangsy
Client: Art Fights Back
Software/Hardware: Adobe Illustrator
Paper/Materials: Mohawk Navajo 80# Cover

0860
Art Director: John Sayles
Designers: John Sayles, Som Inthalangsy
Client: Proctor Mechanical
Software/Hardware: Adobe Illustrator, Quark XPress
Paper/Materials: Luna Matte 60# on Corrugated Box

0894
Art Director: John Sayles
Designers: John Sayles, Som Inthalangsy
Client: United Way
Software/Hardware: Adobe Illustrator, Quark XPress
Paper/Materials: Cougar 80# Cover Screenprinted on Corrugated Box

0901
Art Director: John Sayles
Designers: John Sayles, Som Inthalangsy
Client: Brix
Software/Hardware: Adobe Illustrator
Paper/Materials: Cougar 100# Cover

0958
Art Director: John Sayles
Designers: John Sayles, Som Inthalangsy
Client: Sbemco International
Software/Hardware: Adobe Illustrator, Quark XPress
Paper/Materials: Luna Matte 80# Cover

0981
Art Director: John Sayles
Designers: John Sayles, Som Inthalangsy
Client: Official Airline Guide (OAG)
Software/Hardware: Adobe Illustrator, Quark XPress
Paper/Materials: Cougar Natural 80# Cover

Sayre Gaydos

0097, 0134, 0135, 0175, 0176,0177, 0178, 0189, 0224, 0225, 0226, 0227
Designer: Sayre Gaydos
Client: Ink Farm

0104, 0205
Designer: Sayre Gaydos
Client: Peter Kruty Edition

0544
Designer: Sayre Gaydos
Client: Dadourian & Nelson

0734
Designer: Sayre Gaydos
Client: Kristin Newman Designs

0824
Designer: Sayre Gaydos
Client: Leigh Merinoff

Scott Baldwin

0031, 0032, 0033
Designer: Scott Baldwin
Client: Ironworks Graphic Sign
Software/Hardware: Linocut, Letterpress
Paper/Materials: Exact Matte Cover

0034
Designer: Scott Baldwin
Client: ironworksgraphics.com
Software/Hardware: Linocut, Letterpress
Paper/Materials: Exact Matte Cove

0092
Designer: Scott Baldwin
Client: Scott Baldwin
Software/Hardware: Linocut, Adobe Photoshop

Selbert Perkins Design

0453
Art Director: Clifford Selbert
Designer: Avvi Raquel-Santos
Client: Selbert Perkins Design
Software/Hardware: Adobe Illustrator, Mac
Paper/Materials: Cardboard

0751
Art Director: Sheri Bates
Client: Citizen Schools
Software/Hardware: Quark XPress, Mac
Paper/Materials: Monadnock

0697
Art Directors: Robin Perkins, Clifford Selbert
Designer: Erin Carney
Client: Elizabeth Sachs
Software/Hardware: Mac OS, Adobe Illustrator

0916
Art Directors: Robin Perkins, Clifford
Selbert
Designer: Jessica Bittani
Client: Self Promotion
Software/Hardware: Mac OS, Adobe
Illustrator, Adobe Photoshop, Quark
Xpress

0924
Art Directors: Robin Perkins, Clifford
Selbert
Designer: Ross Geerdes
Client: Anti Gravity
Software/Hardware: Mac OS 9

Shamlian Advertising

0002
Art Director: Fred Shamlian
Designer: Fred Shamlian
Client: Self-Promo
Software/Hardware: Quark XPress,
Adobe Illustrator
Paper/Materials: CD/Claimsbell

0039
Art Director: Fred Shamlian
Designer: Jessica Paolella
Client: The Vague Family
Software/Hardware: Quark XPress,
Adobe Illustrator, Adobe Photoshop
Paper/Materials: Paper, CD, Triangle

Shea, Inc.

0339
Art Director: James Rahn
Designer: James Rahn
Client: Shea, Inc.
Software/Hardware: Adobe Illustrator
Paper/Materials: Curious Metallic

Sibley Peteet Design-Dallas

0195
Art Director: Don Gibley
Designer: Brandon Kirk
Client: Sibley Peteet Design-Dallas
Software/Hardware: Adobe Illustrator,
Photoshop
Paper/Materials: French Construction,
Pure white

0196
Art Director: Don Sibley
Designer: Brandon Kirk
Client: Sibley Peteet Design-Dallas
Software/Hardware: Adobe Illustrator,
Adobe Photoshop, Streamline
Paper/Materials: Mohawk Supreme

0447
Designer: Brandon Kirk
Client: Brandon Kirk, Julia Holcomb
Software/Hardware: Adobe Illustrator,
Quark XPress
Paper/Materials: French Speckle Tone

Simon Does

0187
Art Director: Karen Simon
Designer: Karen Simon
Client: Simon Does
Software/Hardware: Max, Quark XPress,
Adobe Illustrator

Simply Put Design

0534
Art Director: Carrene Tracy
Client: Margaret Jacobi
Software/Hardware: Adobe Photoshop,
Adobe Illustrator
Paper/Materials: Ribbon

0795, 0845
Art Director: Carrene Tracy
Software/Hardware: Adobe Illustrator
Paper/Materials: Strathmore Pastelle

0789
Art Director: Carrene Tracy
Client: Louise Kangas
Software/Hardware: Adobe Illustrator,
Adobe Photoshop
Paper/Materials: Mohawk Superfine

0611
Art Director: Carrene Tracy
Software/Hardware: Adobe Illustrator
Paper/Materials: Mohawk Superfine

SiSu Design

0644
Art Director: Jennifer Stucker
Designer: Jennifer Stucker
Client: Josh & Tonya Alkire
Software/Hardware: Macromedia
Freehand

0645
Art Director: Jennifer Stucker
Designer: Jennifer Stucker
Client: Boys & Girls Clubs of Toledo

Software/Hardware: Macromedia
Freehand
Paper/Materials: Lustro

SK Visual

0128
Art Directors: Katya Lyumkis, Spencer
Lum
Designers: Katya Lyumkis, Spencer Lum
Client: Self-Promotion
Software/Hardware: Adobe Illustrator,
Paper/Materials: Styrofoam Trays,
Tin Cans, Cellophane Wrap, Plastic
Shreds & Tea

Sky Design

0900
Art Director: W. Todd Vaught
Designer: Carrie Wallace
Client: Sky Design
Software/Hardware: Adobe Illustrator
8.0
Paper/Materials: Stamped Aluminum
Coated Paper

Smudge Ink

0182
Designer: Kate Saliba
Paper/Materials: White Cotton Paper

0192
Client: Kate Saliba
Paper/Materials: Rives BFK Tan Paper,
Hand-Carved Linoleum Block

0260, 0261, 0262, 0263, 0322, 0325
Client: Kate Saliba

0307
Designer: Kate Saliba
Client: Private
Paper/Materials: 600 gr. Copper Plate,
Bright White Paper

0422
Designer: Kate Saliba
Client: Private
Paper/Materials: Magnani Pescia Italian
Blue paper

0443
Designer: Kate Saliba
Client: Private
Paper/Materials: Lenox 100% Cotton
Paper

0464
Designer: Kate Saliba
Client: Private
Paper/Materials: 100% Cotton Paper

0819
Designer: Kate Saliba
Client: Private
Software/Hardware: Sewing Machine,
Chandler & Price Letterpress
Paper/Materials: 100% Cotton Lenox
White Paper

Sommese Design

0458, 0988, 0993
Art Directors: Lanny Sommese, Kristin
Sommese
Designer: Lanny Sommese
Client: Sommese Design
Software/Hardware: Adobe Illustrator,
Adobe Photoshop, Mac

0698
Art Directors: Kristin Sommese, Lanny
Sommese
Client: Sommese Design
Software/Hardware: Mac, Adobe
Illustrator, Adobe Photoshop
Paper/Materials: Dancing Forks

Sonsoles Llorens Design

0267
Art Director: Sonsoles Llorens
Designer: Sonsoles Llorens
Client: Sonsoles Llorens Design
Software/Hardware: Macromedia
Freehand, Mac
Paper/Materials: Offset Printing

0244
Art Director: Sonsoles Llorens
Designer: Sonsoles Llorens
Client: Sonsoles Llorens
Software/Hardware: Macromedia
Freehand, Mac
Paper/Materials: Plastic Ball,
Silkscreening, Paper

Special Modern Design

0536
Art Director: Karen Barranco
Designer: Karen Barranco
Client: Sitton Tayler
Software/Hardware: Mac, Adobe
Illustrator, Adobe Photoshop

Paper/Materials: Bark, Tissue, Ribbon, Offset Printing

Splash Interactive

0144
Art Director: Ivy Wong
Designer: Ivy Wong
Client: Splash Interactive
Software/Hardware: Adobe Illustrator, Adobe Photoshop, Mac G4

Stacey Bakaj

0251, 0879
Designer: Stacey Bakaj
Client: Stacey Bakaj
Software/Hardware: Vandercook SP15
Paper/Materials: Letterpress

Stahl Partners, Inc.

0889
Art Director: David Stahl
Client: Stahl Design Inc.
Software/Hardware: Quark XPress,
Paper/Materials: French Paper Duro-Tone, Butcher Off-White

Steff Geissbuhler (Chermayeff & Geismar, Inc.)

0010
Art Director: Steff Geissbuhler
Designer: Steff Geissbuhler
Client: Schneiderman/Geissbuhler
Paper/Materials: Reich Paper, Iridescent Offset & Engraving

0011
Art Director: Steff Geissbuhler
Designer: Steff Geissbuhler
Client: Schneiderman/Geissbuhler
Paper/Materials: Strathmore papers,
Die-Cut & Engraving

0223
Art Director: Steff Geissbuhler
Designer: Steff Geissbuhler
Client: Schneiderman/Geissbuhler
Paper/Materials: Strathmore paper,
Blind Emboss & Engraving

Stephen Burdick Design

0964
Designer: Stephen Burdick
Client: Self-Promotion
Software/Hardware: Adobe Photoshop

Paper/Materials: Inkjet Output

Stereobloc

0662, 0664
Art Director: Holger Stumpe
Designer: Maik Brummundt
Client: Galerie Griedervonpotikamer
Software/Hardware: Quark XPress
Paper/Materials: Profisilk 350 gm 3

0969
Art Director: Udo Albrecht
Designer: Maik Brummundt
Client: Stereobloc
Software/Hardware: Adobe Photoshop,
Quark XPress
Paper/Materials: Cromolux

0975
Art Director: Udo Albrecht
Designer: Udo Albrecht
Client: Stereobloc
Software/Hardware: Adobe Photoshop,
Quark XPress
Paper/Materials: Invercote, Albato
290gm 3

Studio International

0903, 0911
Art Director: Boris Liubicic
Designer: Boris Liubicic
Client: Europe 2020/Minitry RH
Software/Hardware: Corel Draw
Paper/Materials: B/W Dacot 200/g

Studio J

0245
Designer: Angela Jackson
Client: Angela Jackson
Software/Hardware: Adobe Illustrator
Paper/Materials: Spice Jars, Digital
Color Copies

0990
Designer: Angela Jackson
Client: Angela Jackson, Studio J
Software/Hardware: Mac, Adobe
Illustrator
Paper/Materials: Digital Copies,
Homemade Candy

Stults Printing Co.

0923
Art Director: Rachel Stults
Designer: Rachel Stults

Sudduth Design Co.

0138
Art Director: Toby Sudduth
Designer: Toby Sudduth
Client: Personal
Software/Hardware: Adobe Illustrator,
Adobe Photoshop
Paper/Materials: Epson Inkjet

0461
Art Directors: Holly & Toby Sudduth
Designer: Toby Sudduth
Client: Holly & Toby Sudduth
Software/Hardware: Adobe Illustrator
Paper/Materials: 2 Color Letterpress
with Various Photographs

Swirly Designs by Lianne & Paul

0063
Art Director: Lianne Stoddard
Client: Swirly Designs
Software/Hardware: Adobe Illustrator
8.0, Mac
Paper/Materials: Celery Color Cover
Stock & Pink Glitter

0272
Art Director: Lianne Stoddard
Designer: Paul Stoddard
Client: Swirly Designs
Software/Hardware: Adobe Illustrator
8.0, Mac
Paper/Materials: White Texture Cover
Stock, Orange Vellum & Eyelets

t

That's Nice, LLC

0052
Art Director: Nigel Walker
Designer: Erica Heitman
Client: That's Nice LLC
Software/Hardware: Quark XPress,
Adobe Illustrator, Adobe Photoshop

0194
Art Director: Nigel Walker
Designer: Phil Evans
Client: That's Nice, LLC
Software/Hardware: Quark XPress,
Adobe Illustrator, Adobe Photoshop

0875
Art Director: Nigel Walker
Designers: David Phan, Scott
Robertson, Elan Harris

Client: That's Nice, LLC
Software/Hardware: Quark XPress,
Adobe Illustrator, Adobe Photoshop

0886
Art Director: Nigel Walker
Designer: Kaoru Kaojima
Client: That's Nice, LLC
Software/Hardware: Quark XPress,
Adobe Illustrator, Adobe Photoshop

0968
Art Director: Nigel Walker
Designers: Erica Heitman, Scott
Robertson
Client: That's Nice, LLC
Software/Hardware: Quark XPress,
Adobe Illustrator, Adobe Photoshop

The Commissary

0685
Art Director: Lucas Charles
Designer: Alison Charles
Client: Singelyn Family
Software/Hardware: Quark XPress, Mac
Paper/Materials: 80lb Strathmore

0818
Art Director: Lucas Charles
Designer: Alison Charles
Client: Armstrong & Fox Family
Software/Hardware: Quark XPress,
Adobe Illustrator, Mac
Paper/Materials: 60lb Strathmore

0654
Art Director: Lucas Charles
Designer: Lucas Charles
Client: The University of Memphis
Software/Hardware: Adobe Illustrator,
Mac
Paper/Materials: Glassine Envelope, 60
lb. Uncoated

0822
Art Director: Lucas Charles
Designer: Lucas Charles
Client: The Charles & Johnson Family
Software/Hardware: Quark XPress,
Adobe Photoshop, Mac
Paper/Materials: 60lb Strathmore

0492
Art Director: Lucas Charles
Designer: Alison Charles
Client: Hall & Wilson Family
Software/Hardware: Adobe Photoshop,
Quark XPress, Mac
Paper/Materials: French Paper

0834
Art Director: Lucas Charles
Designer: Hudd Byard
Client: Hinshaw & Byard Families
Software/Hardware: Adobe Photoshop,
Quark XPress, Mac
Paper/Materials: Glassine Envelopes,
Wausau Bristol

The Point, LLC

0766
Art Director: Janet Fried
Designer: Janet Fried
Client: Memorial Art Gallery
Software/Hardware: Quark XPress, Mac

0895
Art Director: Janet Fried
Designer: Janet Fried
Client: Syracuse University
Software/Hardware: Quark XPress, Mac

The Post Press

0368, 0387
Art Director: Martha Carothers
Designer: Martha Carothers
Client: The Post Press
Paper/Materials: Rubber Stamp, Hole
Punch

Timespin

0250
Designer: Tino Schmidt
Client: Timespin
Software/Hardware: Macromedia
Freehand, Mac
Paper/Materials: 250g Special Paper,
Opaque Envelope

Tom Fowler, Inc.

0066
Art Director: Brien O'Reilly
Designer: Brien O'Reilly
Client: Brien & Sandi O'Reilly
Software/Hardware: Quark XPress,
Adobe Photoshop
Paper/Materials: Hammermill Laserprint

0433
Art Directors: Brien & Sandi O'Reilly
Designer: Brien O'Reilly
Client: Brien & Sandi O'Reilly
Software/Hardware: Quark XPress,
Adobe Photoshop
Paper/Materials: Mohawk Superfine

0680
Art Director: Tom G. Fowler
Designers: Thomas G. Fowler, Karl S.
Maruyama
Client: Pfizer, Inc.
Software/Hardware: Adobe Illustrator
Paper/Materials: Magic Cube, Pfizer
Holiday Cube

Tong Design Graphic Studio

0001, 0111, 0345
Art Director: Tong Wai Hang
Designer: Tong Wai Hang
Client: Tong Design Graphic Studio
Software/Hardware: Adobe Illustrator
8.0

Top Design Studio

0169
Art Director: Peleg Top
Designer: Peleg Top
Client: Quincy Jones Music Publishing

0346
Art Director: Peleg Top
Designer: Peleg Top
Client: Top Design Studio

0520
Art Director: Peleg Top
Designer: Peleg Top
Client: Crystal Stairs

0592
Art Director: Peleg Top
Designer: Peleg Top
Client: Technicolor Digital Cineman

0606
Art Director: Peleg Top
Designers: Peleg Top/Rebekah Beaton
Client: City of Hope/NCFDIC

0614
Art Director: Peleg Top
Designer: Peleg Top
Client: City of Hope

Towers Perrin

0379
Art Director: Michelle Goodman
Designer: Lavonne Czech
Client: Towers Perrin
Software/Hardware: Mac
Paper/Materials: Beckett, Classic Crest
Illustration: Carolyn Williams

0064
Art Directors: Fawn Roth Winick,
Scott May
Designer: Media Consultants
Client: Towers Perrin
Software/Hardware: Mac, Quark XPress,
Adobe Photoshop, Adobe Illustrator
Paper/Materials: White McCoy Dull
Cover Vellum

Tracy Design

0051
Art Director: Jan Tracy
Designers: Rachel Karaca, Sarah Bray
Client: Tracy Design
Software/Hardware: Adobe Illustrator,
Mac
Paper/Materials: French Speckle Tone
Tin Cans

Transcend

0232
Art Director: Hung Q. Tran
Dosigner: Hung Q. Tran
Client: Allison Donahue
Software/Hardware: Adobe Photoshop,
Quark Xpress

0761
Art Director: Hung Q. Tran
Designer: Hung Q. Tran
Client: Transcend
Software/Hardware: Adobe Photoshop,
Quark XPress

Triana The

0482
Designer: Triana The
Software/Hardware: Macromedia
Freehand
Paper/Materials: Paper Bags

Trudy Cole-Zielanski Design

0936
Art Director: Trudy Cole-Zielanski
Designer: Trudy Cole-Zielanski
Client: Trudy Cole-Zielanski Design
Software/Hardware: Adobe Illustrator,
Mac

Turner Duckworth

0937
Art Directors: Bruce Duckworth, David
Turner

Designer: Mark Waters
Client: Turner Duckworth
Paper/Materials: Various

u

University of San Diego

0650
Art Director: Barbara Ferguson
Designer: Barbara Ferguson
Client: Office of Alumni Relations
Software/Hardware: Quark XPress,
Adobe Photoshop, Adobe Illustrator

UP Creative Design & Advertising Co.

0045
Art Director: Jenny Pai
Designer: Jenny Pai
Client: UP Creative Design & Advertising
Software/Hardware: Adobe Illustrator,
Mac
Paper/Materials: Paper

0112
Art Director: Andy Lee
Designer: Peter Lee
Client: Shin Yeh Restaurant
Software/Hardware: Adobe Illustrator,
Mac
Paper/Materials: Paper

0246
Designer: Javen Lin
Client: Chunghwa Post
Software/Hardware: Adobe Illustrator,
Mac
Paper/Materials: Paper

0476
Designer: Javen Lin
Client: Javen Lin
Software/Hardware: Adobe Illustrator,
Mac
Paper/Materials: Paper

0760
Art Director: Andy Lee
Designer: Andy Lee
Client: Jeff Tung
Software/Hardware: Adobe Illustrator,
Mac
Paper/Materials: Paper & Chinese Know

0763
Art Director: Ben Wang
Designer: Ben Wang

Client: Ben Wang
Software/Hardware: Adobe Illustrator, Mac
Paper/Materials: Paper & Silk

0847
Art Director: Ben Wang
Designer: Ben Wang
Client: Jeffrey Wu
Software/Hardware: Adobe Illustrator, Mac
Paper/Materials: Paper

Uturn Design

0505, 0562, 0597
Art Director: Stephanie Zelman
Client: Boston Public Library Foundation

0572
Art Director: Stephanie Zelman
Client: Karen & Adam Tager

0582, 0745
Art Director: Stephanie Zelman
Client: Boston Stock Exchange

V

Vestigio

0277, 0594
Art Director: Emanuel Barbosa
Designer: Emanual Barbosa
Client: CD.Rom Jeans
Software/Hardware: Macromedia Freehand, Mac
Paper/Materials: Torras Paper

0688
Art Director: Emanuel Barbosa
Designer: Emanual Barbosa
Client: Mantra Discotheque
Software/Hardware: Mac, Macromedia Freehand, Adobe Photoshop
Paper/Materials: Torras

Viñas Design

0020, 0418, 0439, 0618, 0709
Art Director: Jaime Viñas
Designer: Jaime Viñas

Visual Dialogue

0776
Art Director: Fritz Klaetke
Designer: Fritz Klaetke
Client: Isabella Stewart Gardner

Museum
Software/Hardware: Quark XPress
Paper/Materials: Cougar Opaque

0659
Art Director: Fritz Klaetke
Designer: Fritz Klaetke
Client: AIGA Boston
Software/Hardware: Quark XPress, Adobe Photoshop
Paper/Materials: Black Marker, Curious Metallics, Utopia Onex

Visual Solutions

0233
Art Director: Cynthia Anderson
Designer: Cynthia Anderson
Software/Hardware: Quark XPress
Paper/Materials: Curious Paper, Metallic, Light Specs, Glue, Glitter

Voice

0023
Art Director: Scott Carslake
Designer: Scott Carslake
Client: Voice
Software/Hardware: Adobe Photoshop, Mac
Paper/Materials: Tablex, Ink Marker

Vrontikis Design Office

0342, 0950
Art Director: Petrula Vrontikis
Designers: Various
Client: Vrontikis Design Office
Software/Hardware: Various
Paper/Materials: Various

0816
Art Director: Petrula Vrontikis
Designer: Tammy Kim
Client: Global-Dining, Inc.
Software/Hardware: Adobe Illustrator, Mac
Paper/Materials: Various

0708
Art Director: Petrula Vrontikis
Designer: Kim Sage
Client: Global-Dining, Inc.
Software/Hardware: Adobe Illustrator, Mac
Paper/Materials: Various

W

W.C. Burgard Illustration

0172, 0180, 0390
Art Director: W.C. Burgard
Designer: W.C Burgard
Client: W.C. Burgard Xmas Card
Paper/Materials: Acrylic, Collage

0327
Art Director: W.C. Burgard
Designer: W.C. Burgard
Client: W.C. Burgard Xmas Card
Paper/Materials: Pencil, Zipatone

0382
Art Director: W.C. Burgard
Designer: W.C. Burgard
Client: W.C. Burgard Xmas Card
Paper/Materials: Pastel, Collage

Wages Design, Inc.

0602
Art Director: Bob Wages
Designer: Joanna Tak
Client: Antron
Software/Hardware: Adobe Photoshop, Adobe Illustrator, Mac
Paper/Materials: Domtar Sandpiper

0844
Art Director: Bob Wages
Designer: Diane Kim
Client: Antron
Software/Hardware: Adobe Photoshop, Adobe Illustrator, Mac
Paper/Materials: Neenah Classic Crest

0642
Art Director: Bob Wages
Designer: Matthew Taylor
Client: Antron
Software/Hardware: Adobe Illustrator, Mac
Paper/Materials: Printer Stock

0660
Art Director: Bob Wages
Designer: Joanna Tak
Client: Antron
Software/Hardware: Adobe Photoshop, Adobe Illustrator, Mac
Paper/Materials: Neenah Classic Crest

Wallace Church

0200
Art Director: Stan Church
Designer: Stan Church
Client: Stan Church
Software/Hardware: Adobe Illustrator 8.0
Paper/Materials: Classic Crest Paper

0308
Art Director: Stan Church
Designer: Stan Church
Client: Wallace Church, Inc
Software/Hardware: Adobe Illustrator, Mac
Paper/Materials: K. Grafx Printing & Embossing

0444
Art Director: Stan Church
Designer: Stan Church
Client: Wallace Church, Inc.
Software/Hardware: Adobe Illustrator, Mac
Paper/Materials: Classic Crest Paper

0508
Art Director: Stan Church
Designer: Laurence Haggerty
Client: Wallace Church, Inc
Software/Hardware: Adobe Illustrator, Mac,
Paper/Materials: Chinet paper Plates with Rubber Stamp

0612
Art Director: John Bruno
Designers: Clare Reece, Ray Bould
Client: Wallace Church Inc
Software/Hardware: Adobe Illustrator, Mac
Paper/Materials: Kraft Paper, Fortune Telling Fish, Black Linen Envelope

0935
Art Directors: John Bruno, Laurence Haggerty
Designer: Laurence Haggerty
Client: Wallace Church, Inc.
Software/Hardware: Adobe Illustrator 8, Mac
Paper/Materials: Plastic Shrink Wrap, Baseball Stitch with Red Cotton Thread, CD w/ Baseball Music

0989
Art Director: Stan Church
Designer: John Bruno
Client: Wallace Church, Inc.

Software/Hardware: Adobe Illustrator
8.0, Mac
Paper/Materials: Wine Bottle, Turkey
Poppers & Label

Watts Design

0803
Art Director: Peter Watts
Designer: Peter Watts
Client: Australian Cricket Board

Webber Design Werks

0411
Art Director: Sean Webber
Designer: Sean Webber
Client: The Webber Family
Software/Hardware: Adobe Photoshop,
Quark XPress
Paper/Materials: Neenah, Classic
Columns, Indigo 80# Cover,
Hammermill 24# Text

Whitenoise

0193
Art Director: Mark Case
Designer: Juue Turkington
Client: Whitenoise
Software/Hardware: Adobe Illustrator
Paper/Materials: 350 gsm Matt Art Card

White Rhino

0329
Art Director: Dan Greenwald
Designer: Athena Hermann
Client: White Rhino
Software/Hardware: Mac, Quark XPress
Paper/Materials: French Frostone

0687
Creative Director: Dan Greenwald
Designer: Athena Herrmann
Client: Foundry Sports Medicine and
Fitness
Software/Hardware: Mac, Adobe
Illustrator, Quark XPress, Adobe
Photoshop
Paper/Materials: Benefit, Living Tree,
French Carnival

Wing Chan Design

0926
Art Director: Wing Chan
Designers: Wing Chan, Eric Chan,
Ryoichi Yamazaki, Yee-Hwa Kim

Client: Wing Chan Design
Software/Hardware: Quark XPress,
Adobe Photoshop
Paper/Materials: Zanders mega Dull,
100# Cover

Wilson Harvey

0049
Art Director: Paul Burgess
Designers: Paul Burgess, Peter Usher
Client: Chameleon
Software/Hardware: Mac, Quark XPress,
Adobe Illustrator, Adobe Photoshop

0173, 0529
Art Director: Paul Burgess
Designer: Wai Lau
Client: Wilson Harvey
Software/Hardware: Mac, Quark XPress,
Adobe Illustrator, Adobe Photoshop

0438
Art Director: Paul Burgess
Designer: Ben Wood
Client: Charlie & Kate Hoult
Software/Hardware: Mac, Quark XPress,
Adobe Illustrator, Adobe Photoshop

0483
Art Director: Paul Burgess
Designers: Paul Burgess, Richard Baker
Client: Paul Henerdine
Software/Hardware: Mac, Quark XPress,
Adobe Illustrator, Adobe Photoshop

0821
Art Director: Paul Burgess
Designer: Paul Burgess
Client: Kirstin, Paul, Teg
Software/Hardware: Mac, Quark XPress,
Adobe Illustrator, Adobe Photoshop

y

Yee Design

0207
Art Director: Danny Yee
Designers: Danny Yee, Sue Yee
Client: Yee Design
Software/Hardware: Adobe Illustrator
Paper/Materials: Tin

Yee-Ping Cho Design

0155
Designer: Yee-Ping Cho

Client: Delta Graphics
Paper/Materials: C1S Card

0170
Designer: Yee-Ping Cho
Client: Aardvark/Syndicate Press
Software/Hardware: Letterpress
Paper/Materials: Lana Watercolor
100% Cotton

0707
Designer: Yee-Ping Cho
Client: Technicolor
Software/Hardware: Adobe Illustrator,
Mac
Paper/Materials: Neenah Classic Crest

0839
Designer: Yee-Ping Cho
Client: Patti Correll
Software/Hardware: Mac, Adobe
Photoshop, Adobe Illustrator
Paper/Materials: Epson

Z

Zappata Disenadores S.C.

0573
Art Director: Ibo Angulo
Designer: Ibo Angulo
Client: Grupo Expansion (Elle Magazine)
Software/Hardware: Macromedia
Freehand, Adobe Photoshop
Paper/Materials: Couche

0772
Art Director: Ibo Angulo
Designer: Ibo Angulo
Client: Claudine & Holger Stamm
Software/Hardware: Macromedia
Freehand 8.0, Adobe Photoshop
Paper/Materials: Recycled Paper,
Albanene, Cord

0939
Art Director: Ibo Angulo
Designer: Ibo Angulo
Client: Laura Lavalle
Software/Hardware: Macromedia
Freehand 8, Adobe Photoshop
Paper/Materials: Couche

Zeroart Studio

0488
Art Directors: Jo Lo, Loy Yu Hin
Designers: Jo Lo & Nicole Chu
Client: Self Promotion (Wedding Card)

Software/Hardware: Macromedia
Freehand, Mac
Paper/Materials: Card-2/0 grm Art
Paper, Process Color & Material Color
Envelope-100grm White Woodfree
Paper, Pantone Color

ZGraphics, Ltd.

0071, 0404
Art Director: LouAnn Zeller
Designer: Kris Martinez Farrell
Client: Contempo Design
Software/Hardware: Quark XPress,
Adobe Photoshop, Mac
Paper/Materials: Curious Iridescents,
Neenah Classic Crest

0194
Art Director: LouAnn Zeller
Designer: Kris Martinez Farrell
Client: ZGraphics, Ltd
Software/Hardware: Quark Xpress,
Adobe Photoshop
Paper/Materials: CTI Papers,
Constellation Jade Raster, Neenah
Classic Crest, Super
Smooth

0543
Art Director: LouAnn Zeller
Designer: Renee Clark
Client: One Small Voice Foundation
Software/Hardware: Quark XPress,
Adobe Photoshop, Mac
Paper/Materials: Winner Gloss

0546
Art Director: LouAnn Zeller
Designer: Renee Clark
Client: Studio C.
Software/Hardware: Quark XPress,
Adobe Photoshop, Mac
Paper/Materials: Fraser Genesis CTI
Papers Glama

0987
Art Director: LouAnn Zeller
Designer: Renee Clark
Client: ZGraphics, Ltd.
Software/Hardware: Quark XPress,
Adobe Illustrator, Mac
Paper/Materials: Appleton Utopia
Premium

ABOUT THE AUTHOR

Peter King & Company has been developing carefully crafted, concept-driven design for corporate, nonprofit, and individual clients since 1994. The studio's focus on fresh, cost-effective solutions has enabled Peter King & Company to satisfy the communications needs of a wide range of organizations, from global corporations to foundations to entrepreneurial firms.

The studio's services include corporate identity development, web and print communications, book design, packaging, trade show and event design, copywriting, account management services, and print production managment. Peter King & Company is located in Boston's Fort Point area.

To learn more, please visit **www.peterkingandcompany.com**